Creative Learning 3-11
and how we document it

Creative Learning 3-11 and how we document it

edited by
Anna Craft, Teresa Cremin,
Pamela Burnard

Trentham Books
Stoke on Trent, UK and Sterling, USA

Trentham Books Limited

Westview House	22883 Quicksilver Drive
734 London Road	Sterling
Oakhill	VA 20166-2012
Stoke on Trent	USA
Staffordshire	
England ST4 5NP	

First published 2008

British Library Cataloguing-in-Publication Data
A catalogue record for this book is available from the British Library

ISBN: 978 1 85856 410 4

Photographic credits
Front cover image: Canterbury Nursery School and Centre for Families and Children: problem solving, team work and motor skills development through environmental den making. More details at www.canterburycc.co.uk/meaning.php

Back cover, bottom image: Canterbury Nursery School and Centre for Families and Children: story making, self expression and sensory development through light and shadow play. More details at www.canterburycc.co.uk/meaning.php

Remainder of images taken from A Child's Eye research programme, involving children documenting their own learning, supported by Creative Partnerships, Bristol

Photo credits: Kamina Walton. More details at http://www.kaminawalton.co.uk/

Designed and typeset by Trentham Books Limited
Printed and bound in Great Britain by 4edge Limited, Hockley

For those in our lives who operate with mindful love

Contents

Acknowledgements

Many people have contributed to the production of this book. Our thanks are due to the members of the Creativity in Education Special Interest Group in the British Educational Research Association who gave support to the two-day international symposium at the University of Cambridge which inspired the book. To the co-authors with whom we have debated the ideas since, and whose work is produced here, we extend our appreciation. Our thanks are due to the many educators and children with whom we come into contact through our varied work in different parts of the world, whose efforts keep us mindful of the challenges and the opportunities involved in fostering the learning potential of both learners and teachers.

We are also grateful to Gillian Klein at Trentham Books, who saw the potential in the manuscript, to Emma Stewart at Canterbury Christchurch University who kept track of drafts and Linda Nash at The Open University who helped in the final stages. Finally our thanks are due to those closest to us who have witnessed the gestation of this project, whose unfailing support and encouragement is greatly appreciated.

Anna Craft, Teresa Cremin, Pamela Burnard
May 2007

The authors

Abdul Aziz Al-Horr is Director of the Arab Educational Training Centre for Gulf States.

John Baer is Professor of Educational Psychology at Rider University, USA.

Jonathan Barnes is a Senior Lecturer in Education at Canterbury Christ Church University.

Celia Burgess-Macey is a Lecturer in the Department of Educational Studies at Goldsmiths College, London University.

Pamela Burnard is a Senior Lecturer in the Faculty of Education at the University of Cambridge.

Kerry Chappell is a Research Fellow at the University of Exeter. She is affiliated to The Open University and Goldsmiths University of London, also teaching at University of Cambridge, Laban and The Place.

Vivian M Y Cheng is Assistant Professor, Hong Kong Institute of Education.

Ruth Churchill Dower is Director of Isaacs UK, a cultural learning company with a remit to build learning networks across international, cultural and educational communities.

Anna Craft is Professor of Education at the University of Exeter and at The Open University.

Teresa Cremin (formerly known professionally as Teresa Grainger) is Professor of Education (Literacy) at The Open University.

David Henry Feldman is Professor of Developmental Psychology in the Eliot-Pearson Department of Child Development at Tufts University, Medford, Massachusetts, USA.

Genie Gabel-Dunk teaches in two London primary schools, works as an Associate Lecturer for Open University Education and undertakes research.

Gill Hope is a Senior Lecturer in Design and Technology Education at Canterbury Christ Church University.

Bob Jeffrey is Research Fellow at The Open University.

James C Kaufman is Associate Professor at California State University and Director of the Learning Research Institute.

Alexander Loewenthal lectures at Brunel and London Universities, Trinity and Morley Colleges, does school workshops in the UK and abroad and is Calypsonian-in-Residence for the BBC.

Ben Mardell is a researcher at Project Zero, working on the Making Learning Visible Project and Associate Professor at Lesley University, USA.

David S Martin is Professor/Dean Emeritus from Gallaudet University in Washington, D.C. He is currently Adjunct Professor at several universities in the Boston, Massachusetts area.

Salome Otami is an instructor at the University of Education Winneba in Ghana and a Masters candidate at Tufts University, USA.

Günseli Oral is Associate Professor in Akdeniz University, School of Education.

Mahender Reddy Sarsani is Associate Professor of Education, Kakatiya University, India.

Stephen Scoffham is a Principal Lecturer in the Faculty of Education at Canterbury Christ Church University.

Pamela Smyth is the Primary Education Adviser in the London Borough of Bromley.

David Spendlove is a Lecturer in Education at the University of Manchester.

Terri Turner is a researcher at Project Zero, Harvard University.

Keang-Ieng (Peggy) Vong lectures at the Faculty of Education of the University of Macau.

Veronica Wong is a research consultant at The Hong Kong Institute of Education, and Honorary Associate Professor lecturing at the University of Hong Kong.

Dominic Wyse is a Senior Lecturer in the Faculty of Education at the University of Cambridge.

FOREWORD
Documenting creative learning, changing the world

David Henry Feldman

Piaget and Vygotsky were the greatest developmental theorists of the twentieth century. Each had an abiding passion to understand creativity, and both were frustrated in their efforts to comprehend it. Given that two of the best minds of all time were dissatisfied with their insights into creativity, it should be no surprise that we are still having a hard time with it. But what is interesting, and perhaps instructive, is why Piaget and Vygotsky found themselves unable to crack the creativity problem even as they recognised it as the most important problem to crack (Piaget in Bringuier, 1980; Bruner, 1986).

Piaget in one way and Vygotsky in another were constrained by the commitments they made to certain ways of looking at the growth of the mind and the processes central to that growth. For Piaget, logic was so central to his theory that it blocked him from considering other ways of thinking such as intuitive, unconscious and nonlinear that may have proved helpful in his quest. Piaget also made the scientific commitment to study only those mental transformations that are inevitable, that all will achieve, leaving aside the variations and extremes that are probably more relevant to creative transformations (Feldman, Csikszentmihalyi and Gardner, 1994; Piaget in Bringuier, 1980, p39). As a result, Piaget's theory has little light to shed on creativity beyond the inevitable transformations of his four stages (Feldman, 1988).

For Vygotsky, the constraining force was history. As an early proponent of the idealistic, Marxist inspired communist revolution in Russia, Vygotsky saw history as the most central and significant source of explanation for what currently exists and for what is possible. He argued (Vygotsky, 1978) that history was also the key to understanding individual change and transformation: he placed developmental psychology, the most historical of the psychological disciplines, at the heart of psychology itself. As some critics have noted, Vygotsky was naïve and overly trusting of history to produce wise and adaptive changes (Piaget, 1995), leaving him unable to shed light on great moments of change that defy history or appear to be largely independent of historical influence (e.g. Bruner, 1986). His invocation of the Marxist principle of spontaneity was little more than a label for changes that appear to be un-constrained by history (Bruner, 1986). Thus Vygotsky had little to contribute to what we know about creativity in spite of being deeply involved in the critical analysis of poetry and literature as a young scholar (Vygotsky, 1971).

What is instructive about these two examples is the tension between what the theorists had learned and what they hoped to do with their hard won knowledge (Weisberg, 1999). The features that were the greatest sources of strength and heuristic power in their theories prevented them from using their understanding of logic and of history to uncover powerful creative transformations. For Piaget, '[The] crux of my problem is to try to explain how novelties are possible and how they are formed' (Piaget, 1971, p194) and this was his greatest unmet challenge. For Vygotsky, how to reconcile the necessity of instruction, support, guidance and a vision of where things are supposed to go with a spirit of rebellion that defied all of these, was beyond him. He died at 36 so we will never know how his thinking might have developed.

We should not be discouraged if our vision of creativity is not clear. Docu-menting creative learning is a noble goal even if it is not completely clear what we mean by documenting, creative or learning. The goal of this volume, to understand the 'what', 'how' and 'why' of creative learning is now being pursued in many parts of the world and reflects many ways to try to docu-ment creative learning as it is identified in each cultural context and through each society's web of meaning.

Based on the fine contributions to this collection, it is clear that good work can be done that is relevant to, if not clearly guided by, a vision of creative learning. It may be that an evolving, working definition of 'creative learning' such as those offered by Anna Craft (2005), Bob Jeffrey (this volume) or David Spendlove and Dominic Wyse (this volume) are good enough to keep the work going. The research groups and practitioners contributing to this volume have brought their considerable skills to bear on documenting, through a range of approaches, what is going on when creative learning happens.

In this brief foreword I suggest some preliminary distinctions that may help to unpack and order the dimensions of our target of developing creative learning, and guide our efforts with policy, research, practice and also theory. If the distinctions prove useful, they may also help to guide efforts towards clearer and more transparent documentation of what is happening, how it happens and why it works or fails to work. The key dimensions of the problem are the three terms *creative, learning* and *development.* By specifying even in a preliminary way what we mean by each of these and how they relate to each other, we may make some progress (Gruber and Davis, 1988).

For the term creative we need to differentiate between and among its various forms (Gardner, 1993; Sternberg, 2003), to recognise the significance of cultural context in defining it (Craft, 2005) and distinguish what is distinctive about creativity compared with concepts such as innovation, imagination, spontaneity, openness, playfulness and intuition. There is no best way to conceptualise the meaning of creative learning, nor is there a best way to document it.

It may be helpful to start with the intentional effort to transform that is at the heart of a creative contribution, as well as on the outcome (Feldman, 1988). What makes an effort potentially creative is the intention to change the world in some way, while what makes it creative is that it is judged to have done so (Feldman, Csikszentmihalyi and Gardner, 1994). There are many possible ways to encourage the desire to change the world in small or large ways, but unless there is intent, and unless the outcome of the effort has produced a worthwhile change, another term is probably more appropriate than creativity. The 'what, how and why' of creativity as a distinct process therefore includes a dissatisfaction with things as they are and a notion which has been brought to fruition about how to change them for the better.

Learning is more difficult to specify than creativity. For the purposes of our effort to bring creativity into the daily practice and experience of education, it may be productive to think of learning as the acquisition of the information, skill, technology and techniques that enable creativity. Of itself, what is learned is not creative. Indeed, in the Vygotsky and Piaget examples, what they had learned *prevented* them from being able to give a transformational, powerful explanation of creativity. Looking at learning this way suggests that there may be no such thing as creative learning *per se.* There is learning that may enable creative work and learning that may prevent creative work from occurring. Which kinds of learning experiences for which kinds of students enable creativity rather than blocking it, and how these occur, is one of the major challenges of the international effort now underway and is reflected in the chapters of this book.

Development depends on qualitative changes that enhance the broad capabilities of the student both to learn new information and to make creative and valued transformations. It is also marked by transformations in the valued domains that are the target of creative efforts (Feldman, 1988). Studying how development works (Feldman, 1986) may help to guide our understanding of creativity as a qualitative transformation of a valued domain (Sawyer and John-Steiner, 2003), while studying creativity may further our understanding of what we mean by development (Feldman, 2003; Sawyer, 2003). Development is at the heart of the movement, but should not be confused with more humble practices or more mundane changes. Development is major. So development may be what is desired, but being clear about what development means is necessary for specifying how to promote it, and why its significance in the educative process is justified.

The many and varied contributions to this important volume can be seen as seeking to deepen understanding and transform practice in education toward more creative learning and development in our children, and to develop the documentation practices through which we can evaluate our efforts. Clearly, the 'what, how and why' of creative learning and its documentation will demand our best efforts for years to come. To succeed in enhancing creative learning for the children of the world is the equivalent of trying to fly an aeroplane at the same time as it is being designed, built, and tested. Piaget and Vygotsky would no doubt be impressed.

(My thanks to the editors for their helpful comments on this Foreword)

References

Bringuier, J-C (1980) *Conversations with Jean Piaget.* Chicago: University of Chicago Press

Bruner, J (1986) *Actual minds, possible worlds.* Cambridge, MA: Harvard University Press

Craft, A R (2005) *Creativity in schools: tensions and dilemmas.* Oxford: RoutledgeFalmer

Feldman, D H (1986) How development works. In I Levin (ed) *Stage and structure: reopening the debate* (p284-306). Norwood NJ: Ablex

Feldman, D H (1988) Universal to unique: toward a cultural genetic epistemology. *Archive de Psychologie* 56 p271-279

Feldman, D H (2003) The creation of Multiple Intelligences Theory: a study in high-level thinking. In R K Sawyer and V John-Steiner (eds) *Creativity and development* (p139-185). Oxford: Oxford University Press

Feldman, D H, Csikszentmihalyi, M and Gardner, H (1994) *Changing the world: A framework for the study of creativity.* Westport, CT: Greenwood Press

Gardner, H (1993) *Creating minds.* New York: Basic Books

Gruber, H and Davis, S (1988) Inching our way up Mount Olympus: the evolving systems approach to creative thinking. In R Sternberg (ed) *The nature of creativity* (p243-270) Cambridge UK: Cambridge University Press

Piaget, J (1971) The theory of stages in cognitive development, in D Green, M Ford and G Flamer (eds) *Measurement and Piaget* (p1-11, also p194). New York: McGraw-Hill

Piaget, J (1995) Comments on Vygotsky's criticisms of Language and Thought of the Child and Judgment and Reasoning in the Child. *New Ideas in Psychology* 13 p325-340 (originally published in 1962)

Sawyer R K (2003) Emergence in creativity and development. In R K Sawyer, R K and V John-Steiner (eds) *Creativity and development* (p12-60). Oxford: Oxford University Press

Sawyer, R K and John-Steiner, V (eds) (2003) *Creativity and development.* Oxford: Oxford University Press

Sternberg, R J (2003) The development of creativity as a decision-making process. In R K Sawyer and V John-Steiner (eds) *Creativity and development* (p91-138). Oxford: Oxford University Press

Vygotsky, L (1971) *The psychology of art.* Cambridge, MA: MIT Press (originally published in Russian in 1922)

Vygotsky, L (1978) *Mind in society.* Cambridge, MA: Harvard University Press

Weisberg, R W (1999) Creativity and knowledge: a challenge to theories. In R J Sternberg (ed) *Handbook of creativity* (p226-250). Cambridge, UK: Cambridge University Press

OPENING REMARKS
Creative learning: an emergent concept

Anna Craft, Teresa Cremin, Pamela Burnard

Since the mid 1990s, creativity in education has experienced an unprecedented resurgence of activity as an area of scholarship, as a key element of the official agenda and in relation to classroom practice.

Policy makers, practitioners and researchers, from their different perspectives, have undertaken much work in theorising numerous aspects of this field. Some is conceptual (Craft, 2002, Spendlove and Wyse, 2005), some on teacher perspectives (Woods and Jeffrey, 1996, Burnard, 2004), some on teaching creatively in universities (Grainger, Barnes and Scoffham, 2004) and some around pupil perspectives (Jeffrey, 2006, Burnard, 2004) and on classroom practicalities (Beetlestone, 1998, Duffy, 2006). Other work has focused on analysing why the re-emergence has occurred (Craft, 2005, 2006). The resurgence of interest spans numerous cultures including Europe, the Middle East, far East and China, Australasia and North America.

Creative learning: the emergence of a discourse
In the 21st century, the notion of creative learning, which is distinct from but related to both creativity and learning, surfaced in England, and is used increasingly commonly by classroom practitioners, policy makers and researchers. It emerged in the midst of efforts to re-ignite creativity in education as vital to cultural and economic development, and can be traced to the government-commissioned report of the National Advisory Committee on Creative and Cultural Education (NACCCE, 1999). This recommended a core role within the curriculum for creativity, in terms of both learning and pedagogy. It synthesised empirical work undertaken by researchers such as Woods and Jeffrey during the 1990s, distinguishing between creative teaching and teaching for creativity. It recommended closer partnerships between schools

and creative and cultural organisations, a proposal which was funded from 2002 by government in the form of Creative Partnerships.

Creative learning linked to creative and cultural education?

Operating now in 36 regions of urban and rural deprivation across England, the Creative Partnerships programme supports teachers and creative and cultural partners in long-term partnerships focused on fostering the creativity of students aged 5-16. One third of all schools in England have had some engagement with the programme since its inception, and research tracking pupil progress suggested that by 2006 children across the age span who have had some contact with the programme out-performed those who have not (NFER, 2006). A national review of the programme undertaken by the government inspection agency (Ofsted, 2006) endorsed this finding, noting that projects had provided rich inspiration for learners, fostering creative skills such as risk-taking, improvisation, resilience and collaboration, and contributing to raised confidence and aspirations.

The programme has increasingly involved reflection in action and action-research in the partnerships. The enquiry model lies at the heart of a wider roll-out of this partnership work, through the Creative Action Research Awards (CARA), involving teachers, external partners and mentors in tri-angular, long term enquiry focusing on creative learning (CapeUK, 2006). From these programmes emerged the twin foci of impact on pupil learning and tracking changes in pedagogy.

The mission of the Creative Partnerships programme is to 'develop and main-stream creative teaching and learning' (Creative Partnerships, 2007). It reports difference in expectations, language and practices brought to the classroom by external creative and cultural partners, which can challenge and stretch both pupils and teachers, as well as benefit the partners them-selves (*ibid*). Whilst exploration of these dimensions is on-going within the programme, evaluation from Ofsted (2006) alongside the findings on shifts for learners, identified a clear increase in teachers' skills and creativity in fostering creative learning.

This activity and its outcomes provide an interesting contrast with some of the performative approaches to education which have been widespread since the late 1980s internationally (Ball, 2003; Boxley, 2003; White, 2006).

At its heart, is a conceptualisation of creative learning, which is seen as alter-ing pedagogy in highlighting innovation, and as having the potential to prompt change within schools, across the curriculum and within the wider community.

Whilst the programme seeks to build partnership capacity in both schools and creative and cultural sectors in working effectively together and to display and disseminate methodologies for creative learning, the meaning of creative learning is still evolving. Effectively it is the middle ground between creative teaching and teaching for creativity (Jeffrey and Craft, 2004). Its meaning remains contested and blurred, although attempts to conceptualise it are both necessary and of significance. Building on the NACCCE (1999) definition, highlighting both imagination and experience, and drawing also on the work of Spendlove and Wyse (2005), a recent definition (Craft *et al*, 2006) proposed creative learning as

> significant imaginative achievement as evidenced in the creation of new knowledge as determined by the imaginative insight of the person or persons responsible and judged by appropriate observers to be both original and of value as situated in different domain contexts. (*ibid*, p77)

A further recent definition from work in secondary schools, highlights the imaginative element (Hobbs, 2007) in placing high value on pupils' ideas in combination with experience and emphasising the impact of this on learning itself. Hobbs suggests that creative learning has the potential to engage and motivate pupils, helping them to become increasingly independent, whether learning individually or with others. Creative learning may therefore be understood as 'the use of imagination and experience to develop learning' (*ibid*, p1).

The balance between creativity and learning is also highlighted by Jeffrey (2006), who proposes a slightly different understanding, emphasising the special, combined dimensions of *creativity* suggesting the involvement of pupils in experimentation, innovation and invention, and *learning* suggesting intellectual enquiry. Craft (2005) also highlights the role of learning, suggesting that where learning is understood as construction of meaning, the distinctions between creativity and learning are very fine.

A contested area

As this variety of understandings underline, conceptualisations of creative learning as a term are emergent, and shared understandings of what it could mean, are in evolution (Craft, 2005). Studies exploring creative learning have on the whole been informed by social constructivist models of meaning making, and some are situated in a learning context which is free of the partnership model (Jeffrey and Woods, 2003).

Some researchers have emphasised individualised perspectives (Eglinton, 2003, Burnard *et al*, 2006, Cremin *et al*, 2006, Jeffrey and Craft 2004). In contrast others (Miell and Littleton, 2004) have emphasised collaborative creativity.

Whether drawn from partnership, or from classrooms where partnership forms no part, and whether emphasising individual engagement or collective practices, it is pupil *behaviours* which are the focus. From 2001, these were explored in 120 schools by the Qualifications and Curriculum Authority in England, leading ultimately to the identification of five behavioural elements of creative learning:

- asking questions
- making connections
- imagining what might be
- exploring options
- reflecting critically

(QCA, 2005, 2007).

What is highlighted by seeing creativity as a set of behaviours, and by understanding creative learning as both creativity and learning, is the question of how a classroom practitioner is able to track children's progress. How can we document creative learning is a question with international resonance, particularly in relation to the Italian pre-schools in Reggio Emilia.

The impetus for writing this book is to respond to this question, and to explore both the nature of creative learning for children aged 3-11, and how children's learning may be tracked and understood. The book brings together a range of practitioners and researchers, to explore *what* creative learning and its documentation is, to share perspectives on *how* it is fostered and documented, and to ask *why* fostering and documenting it may be important within education.

An international quest

In Spring 2005, some authors in this volume came together in England from Europe, North America and the Far East for a research symposium hosted at Cambridge University, to conceptualise and extend the what, how and why of the twin questions of the nature of creative learning in children aged 3 to 11, and how it is documented. Since then, others have joined the enquiry, setting this exploration in an international frame, interrogating the interface between creative learning and cultural context, to deepen our understanding of the potential of this term and its attendant pedagogies in varied contexts.

The authors in this volume reflect work being undertaken in Europe, Asia, the middle and far East and North America. In keeping with the co-participative and democratic approach of the editorial group, the authors include practitioner-researchers as well as those based in universities.

The book is organised in three parts: the first addresses the question of what creative learning is, part two asks how creative learning and its documentation happens, and the final part asks why creative learning and its documentation is so important.

In their concluding remarks the editors seek to delineate boundaries to the map, to synthesise the themes raised and to suggest dimensions which may need further exploration, as practitioners, researchers and policy makers seek a better understanding of the what, how and why of creative learning 3-11 and how we document it.

References

Ball, S J (2003) The teacher's soul and the terrors of performativity. *Journal of Education Policy* 18(2) p215-28 Mar-April

Beetlestone, F (1998) *Creative children, imaginative teaching.* Buckingham: Open University Press

Boxley, S (2003) Performativity and Capital in Schools. In *Journal for Critical Education Policy Studies*, 1 (1) http://www.jceps.com/index.php?pageID=articleandarticleID=3 (May, 2007)

Burnard, P (2004) Creativity and pupil-teacher voices in education,. Paper at *British Educational Research Association Conference*, Manchester, England, September 2004

Burnard, P, Craft, A and Grainger, T (2006) Possibility Thinking. In *International Journal of Early Years Education*, 14 (3) p243-262

CapeUK (2006) Creative Action Research Awards http://www.capeuk.org/programmes/cara.html (May, 2007)

Craft, A (2002) *Creativity and Early Years Education.* London: Continuum

Craft, A (2005) *Creativity in Schools: Tensions and Dilemmas.* Oxford: RoutledgeFalmer

Craft, A (2006) Creativity and Wisdom? *Cambridge Journal of Education,* 36(3) p336-350

Craft, A, Grainger, T, Burnard, P and Chappell, K (2006) *Progression in Creative Learning* (PICL Pilot): A study funded by Creative Partnerships. http://www.creative-partnerships.com/research andevaluation/researchAndEvaluationProjects (May 2007)

Creative Partnerships (2007), website http://www.creative-partnerships.com/researchand evaluation/ – last visited 14.05.07

Cremin, T, Burnard, P, and Craft, A (2006). Pedagogy and possibility thinking in the early years. In *International Journal of Thinking Skills and Creativity* 1(2), p108-119

Duffy, B (2006) (2nd edition) *Creative Children, Imaginative Teaching,* Buckingham: Open University Press

Eglinton, K.A. (2003) *Art in the Early Years.* London: RoutledgeFalmer

Grainger, T., Barnes, J.. and Scoffham, S., (2004) A Creative Cocktail: creative teaching in initial teacher education, In *Journal of Education and Teaching* Vol. 38 (3)p 243-253

Hobbs, J. (2007) Why is Creative Learning So Important? Specialist Schools and Academies Trust http://www.schoolsnetwork.org.uk/Article.aspa?PageId=220405andNodeId=357 (May, 2007)

Jeffrey, B (ed) (2006) *Creative Learning Practices: European Experiences.* London: Tufnell Press

Jeffrey, B and Craft, A (2004) Teaching Creatively and Teaching for Creativity: Distinctions and Relationships. In *Educational Studies,* 30 (1) p77-87

Jeffrey, B and Woods, P (2003) *The Creative School: A framework for success, quality and effectiveness,* London: RoutledgeFalmer

Miell, D and Littleton, K (eds) (2004) *Collaborative Creativity: Contemporary Perspectives.* London: Free Association Books

National Advisory Committee on Creative and Cultural Education (NACCCE) (1999) *All Our Futures: Creativity, Culture and Education.* London: Department for Education and Employment

National Foundation for Educational Research (NFER) (2006) The longer term impact of creative partnerships on the attainment of young people. http://www.creative-partnerships.com/content/researchAndEvaluationProjects/153531/?version=1 (May, 2007)

Ofsted (2006) Ofsted inspection of creative partnerships. http://www.creative-partnerships.com/aboutcp/businessevidence (May, 2007)

Qualifications and Curriculum Authority (QCA) (2005) *Creativity: Find it, promote It! – Promoting pupils' creative thinking and behaviour across the curriculum at key stages 1, 2 and 3 – practical materials for schools.* London: Qualifications and Curriculum Authority

Qualifications and Curriculum Authority (QCA) (2007) website: http://www.ncaction.org.uk/creativity/about.htm

Spendlove, D. and Wyse, D (2005) Definitions and barriers: teachers' perceptions of creative learning. Paper presented at *Documenting Creative Learning Symposium: What, How and Why?* University of Cambridge, April 2005

White, J (2006) Arias of learning: creativity and performativity in Australian teacher education. *Cambridge Journal of Education,* 36 (3) p435-453

Woods, P and Jeffrey, B (1996) *Teachable moments: The art of creative teaching in primary schools,* Buckingham: Open University Press

PART ONE
INTRODUCTION
What is creative learning?

Pamela Burnard, Teresa Cremin, Anna Craft

The assumptions which underpin the concept of creative learning, what creative learning is, why promoting it is a necessity not an option, how it is applied by and to individuals or groups of people in different cultures, communities, institutions and societies, depends on how the concept is grounded and practiced and in what context. A fruitful and rigorous way of addressing this concept is to identify and explain just what creative learning is and to explore various ways of documenting it from different perspectives.

Briefly mapping the research on creativity is important in relation to what constitutes creative learning, and how we go about documenting it, by surfacing assumptions that underpin different methodologies and methods. Traditional perspectives from the 1950s witnessed psychological approaches focusing on genius and giftedness within the individual. Psychometric approaches which relied on paper and pencil assessments that tested divergent thinking, cognitive fluency, flexibility, and the originality of a subject's responses dominated the field from 1950 to 1970. For example, the Torrance Tests of Creative Thinking were widely used to identify individuals, including children, who were supposedly creative. This focus on genius and giftedness continued throughout the 1960s as a major period of creativity research particularly in the United States of America. Since the mid 1970s, the field of creativity studies has moved away from testing and towards the study of cognitive, emotional, personal and cultural aspects of creativity, primarily in adults.

More recently, an explosion of creativity research in education has occurred, an ever increasing body of literature providing clear and concrete evidence of

1

the importance of creativity across all aspects of school and adult education. In the UK, in particular, there is vigorous debate and publicity around what creative learning is. This is manifest in the recent development and release in England of the policy framework *Creativity Find it Promote it!* which is proposed for identifying and promoting creativity within the statutory curriculum for children from pre-school age through to the age of sixteen.

The key differences between the chapters in Part One flow from each author's starting point in examining creativity in a specific domain, and the complex range of factors that are directly addressed and acknowledged. For Oral, what creative learning is in different cultural environments depends on how teachers engage in the creative learning process and evaluate each child's unique abilities separately. For Spendlove and Wyse, the way creative learning is defined and understood is determined by the context of the creative learning practice for which the starting point is enquiry and the end point is change.

Looking through the cultural lens of China, Vong reports creative learning as being characterised by practitioners' interpretations of learning and creativity. Here creative learning occurs in relation to much wider cultural values, policies and practices in China. Similarly, Sarsani highlights distinct differences between Western-influenced government-based policy statements and an Eastern tradition which values conformity, hierarchy and didactic approaches to teaching and learning. This theme is echoed in the discussion of teachers' views of creativity in India. For Sarsani, creative learning is not part of the discourse but a term conflated with creative teaching in the discourses of both the teachers and researchers.

Kaufman and Baer examine the role of creative learning from an American perspective on the debates on domain specificity versus the generalisability of creative learning as perceived by teachers. In the final chapter in this section, Martin takes issue with some of the positivist and postmodern contradictions and argues the case for research using mixed methods, critical enquiry and from a practitioner perspective.

When the chapters in this section are taken together, the issues of author position, standpoint and of the starting points they adopt in researching creative learning are apparent. Several authors offer provocations to readers to reconsider cultural meanings and those understandings that are normally taken for granted in our beliefs about creative learning. This is important in understanding creative learning, not least because of a point made strongly by all of the writers – that how we understand creative learning depends upon the theoretical approach taken, and the cultural assumptions which underpin this.

1

Creative learning and culture

Günseli Oral

This chapter explores the role and position of creativity within cultural variations. It is impossible to discuss all aspects of a culture, like orientation toward time, change, acquisition, persistence, rewards, relationships and roles, and the nature and type of skills valued in creative outcomes. Consequently it focuses on the basic factors to consider when dealing with creative learning in different cultural environments.

Culture is defined as 'the total lifestyle of a people, including all the ideas, symbols, preferences, and material objects that they share' (Marcus *et al*, 1996). Creative learning implies facilitating youngsters to enhance their creative skills and helping them reach self-actualisation by allocating resources in a supportive way. In this way, human and financial resources, knowledge and cultural background variables are perceived as integrated parts of the learning atmosphere, which must be exploited creatively.

Culture is an important ingredient of creative learning. Although creativity involves universal aspects, the impact of culture on creative outputs cannot be ignored. Yet, when big or little c creativity in plastic arts are examined in different cultures, similarities between symbols and form-colour relationships in paintings, sculptures and hand crafts can be observed (Oral, 2006; Aksoy, 1996). Similarly, literature in different periods and cultures reflects archetypes (Whitmont, 1969). Some examples of archetypic characters in literature are observed in myths of different cultures and times. For example Gilgamesh in the Ancient Sumerian culture is the oldest character with supernatural powers. He uses his powers to save humans. Hercules in Greek mythology has the same characteristics. In ancient Turkish culture before and during the early periods of Islam Oğuz Khan, Dede Korkut and Abdal Musa had supernatural powers and used their powers for good. Robin Hood in the medieval era in England, and Neo, in the 21st century movie The Matrix, share the same characteristics.

The concept of witches is also observed in ancient Turkish mythology: witches in Turkish myths are known as the 40 women who kidnapped girls and trained them. Amazons are observed to have similar philosophy to the female-dominant world. Leyla and Mecnun or Aslı and Kerem are the Turkish archetypes of lovers who were not lucky enough to reach each other, like Romeo and Juliet. The same topic has been a good source for scenarios for Hollywood today. These and hundreds of other examples of archetypes in arts and cultures, at whatever time and place, demonstrate that humankind shares common symbols.

However, when different cultures are investigated anthropologically, significant differences in their value systems, political views, and educational priorities are apparent. It seems that the life experiences of communities lead to cultural variations in thought and action. One explanation for this is that cultures do not have the same physical and environmental opportunities. This explanation emphasises the chance factor but it would be inadequate to evaluate the cultural variations with the chance factor, for although physical conditions influence a society's future, they are may not be the major determinant of the quality of life in that society all the time. Even in equal geographical positions with equal resources, the way values, norms, institutions and artifacts are perceived and utilised might differ in communities.

Thus there seem to be other factors which affect cultural development. Evolutionary psychologists explain that problem solving and adaptation mechanisms play crucial roles in the survival of a culture. Each culture develops its own survival mechanisms through language acquisition, fear and protection, gender stereotypes and sexuality, morality and cooperation (Cohen, 1985; Kim, 2001).

Richard Dawkins (2000) proposed the idea of meme complexes as important determinants of evolution of creativity through cultures. Dawkins claims that ideas evolve in a similar way to genes. They are transmitted through the units of imitation. Dawkins calls these units meme complexes. Ideas, basics of arts, architecture, and similar cultural performances are transmitted from one mind to another through meme complexes. Dawkins claims that, similar to genes which propagate themselves from body to body through sperms and ova, memes propagate themselves from brain to brain via a process of imitation. This approach offers an interesting framework for creative learning and development in different cultures. Dawkins explains the meme complexes in the following passage:

> Memes grow and spread in natural selection, similar to our genes. Selection favours memes which exploit their cultural environment to their advantage. This cultural environment consists of other memes which are also being selected. The meme pool therefore gains attributes of an evolutionary stable set, which new memes find it hard to invade... (Dawkins, 2000, p143).

A particular set of memes construct new blocks of ideas: new trends, beliefs, religions, life styles, views and policies in arts, science and technology. It is these strong meme complexes which make it difficult to accept and accommodate to new ideas, approaches and even theories, unless they become strong enough to penetrate into the existing meme complexes. Dawkins' approach can be taken as a continuation of Jung's collective unconscious theory (Jung, 1970). Archaic symbols which are shared in our collective unconscious have been re-defined as meme complexes which shape cultural variations in humankind.

Cultural belief systems and their influence on creativity

Among psychological factors underlying creative learning, cultural belief systems have special importance. Individualism and collectivism impact on the nature and nurture of creativity. Individualism is defined as a preference for a loosely knit social framework in society in which individuals are supposed to take care only of themselves and their immediate families (Bhargava, 1992). Industrial and post-industrial societies have individualistic philosophies in which characteristics such as self-discipline, self-sufficiency, personal accountability, and autonomy are highly valued in a person (Kim, Triandis, Kagitcibasi, Choi, and Yoon, 1994).

Collectivism is a contrasting philosophy to individualism. It proposes a tightly knit social framework in which individuals can expect their relatives or other members of their social group to look after them in exchange for unquestioning loyalty (Franzoi, 2000). In collective systems, individuals are evaluated and respected according to their loyalty to the group to which they belong. Research demonstrates that western cultures emphasise and reinforce individualism more whereas non-western cultures reinforce collectivistic values (Marcus, Kitayama and Heiman 1996; Marcus and Kitayama, 1991; Üskül, Hynie and Lalonde, 2004; Carpenter and Karakitapoğlu-aygün, 2005; Ayçiçeği and Haris, 2003).

How is creativity influenced by individualistic and collectivistic cultures? Research suggests that creativity is encouraged and nurtured more in individualistic cultures than collectivistic cultures. Generally, individualistic cultures encourage individual creativity by placing more emphasis on individual views and ideas, regardless of group norms (Shane, 1992; Goncalo and Staw, 2006).

In collectivistic educational systems where group norms and values are superimposed on young people, creative and intellectual skills are shaped by authorities who are obliged to maintain the *status quo*. Thus in collectivistic systems, group cohesion is emphasised and, in many cases, it becomes the strongest motive behind educational policies. Students learn to obey rules and internalise social norms during elementary school years. Those who think or act differently from the rest of the group are perceived as non-conformists by their teachers (Günçer and Oral, 1993). The specific role of education in creative learning is discussed in the following section.

The role of education for creative learning and creative evolution in different cultures

The influence of educational policies and curricula on creative learning

Culture controls our thinking styles and our feelings. We develop a perspective on the world via experiences which we and our ancestors get from the environment, develop value systems emerging from our experiences and transmit them to young people. Gradually, we create cultural identities which come from unique life experiences and develop our cultural structure through generations.

As education plays an important role in cultural development, the quality of educational policies needs special focus. Should we protect our cultural values in education? Should we insist on change? How can we decide on the optimum balance between these extremes?

In individualistic cultures where each person's development is shaped by their own unique characteristics, educational philosophies are person-oriented. Individuals in such cultures equate their values with their individual actions and believe that whatever they do will change the present and the future. However, in collectivist cultures where group values overlap individual potential, the philosophy is oriented towards the importance of the group. These cultures emphasise group values and may ignore the importance of individual potential for the present and future. In collectivistic cultures, educational objectives aim to educate youngsters to become future conformist citizens who will protect the *status quo*, while people in individualistic cultures are educated to become individuals who will create innovations for the present and the future, modifying societal rules according to current conditions and developmental needs.

Education in collectivistic cultures might be regarded as a means for political decision makers to establish their ideologies through future generations. Power groups with a particular belief and ideology can establish formal and informal educational institutions to make their beliefs dominant in future generations. Conflicts may arise between religious and secular schools, or controversies between public schools emphasising national values and missionary schools emphasising the values of foreign cultures. These schools have sometimes opposing missions and aims, which create polarisation in the culture, and this may lead to sub-cultures who resist each other's values and ethical priorities, which affects the learning of young children. Conflicting sub-cultures seek to spread their ideologies through collectivist systems which require the unconditional loyalty of their members.

The role of teacher characteristics in creative learning

Teachers play two roles in the educational process. First, they are expected to facilitate learning environments with opportunities for students to discover their individual talents and develop these talents into skills for working towards self-actualisation. Second, teachers are perceived as role models who encourage students to become creative individuals in society. Therefore, teachers themselves are expected to acquire creative thinking skills. However, this may not, in practice, be the case much of the time. In earlier times, the role of teachers was perceived to be primarily as agents of bureaucratic state expansion or religious power (Gillingham, 2006; Masanori, 1998; Shkedi and Horenczyk, 1995). Socrates was accused of instigating the opposition of his students to the ideological and religious values of the state (Bruell, 1999). Even today, teachers in most countries are manipulated to implement the curriculum which is based on the values and ideologies emphasised by the government.

Teachers may face conflicts between the limitations of the cultural framework and universal educational aims. This is paradoxical, because teachers are also important contributors to the creation of culture. In cases where teachers are involved in a particular cultural background for a long time, they may fail to separate their professional identities from their cultural commitments or identities. Thus they may perceive, evaluate and judge about children's

7

		EMOTIONAL			
		Optimistic			
PERCEPTUAL	Distorted	■ Failure to notice real talents in real amounts; overindulging students ■ Overemphasising student creativity; too much reward for ordinary products ■ Establishing unreal aims and losing time to reach them e.g., insisting on piano lessons for children with little or no interest or talent *Subjective evaluation of products,* *Distorted perception of talents,* *Real creativity left unnoticed.*	■ Identification of talents correctly ■ Facilitation of the learning environment through resource management ■ Searching for the ways of developing potential based on continuous and objective observation and universal values of behaviour *Creative learning,* *Self actualisation,* *Developing creative potential into ideas,* *Solutions and products in society.*	Correct	PERCEPTUAL
		■ Inadequate or missing data about creativity ■ Failure to develop creative potential into skills or products ■ Misconceptualising creative characteristics as threats for the existence of status-quo ■ Devaluation of creativity ■ Punishing creativity or enforcing creative students to conform majority *Meaningless fear of novelty,* *Failure to utilise creative potential in society,* *Resistance against innovations and change.*	■ Perceiving all talents correctly but giving priority only on those required most by society (e.g., pushing a musically gifted child into medicine because it's more respectable in society) *Failure of self- actualisation,* *Conformity to cultural expectations and needs,* *Neglecting creative needs and potential.*		
		Pessimistic			
		EMOTIONAL			

Figure 1.1: The Perceptual-Emotional Model of Teacher Reactions to Creative Outputs

developmental characteristics within the boundaries of that culture (Celep and Bülbül, 2003; Gordon 1999).

Conflicts between a teacher's cultural surrounding and universal educational objectives influence their perceptions and emotions about everyday creativity in the classroom. Perceptual and emotional processes go on most of the time in daily lives but I believe that they have different influences on teachers' actions (see Figure 1.1: Perceptual-Emotional Model).

The first dimension of the model includes teachers' perceptions of creative development. We perceive the world through our individual schemas, which are derived from our experiences and observations. Experiences based on facts and knowledge lead us to frame perception. When teachers have inadequate schemas about creativity due to inadequate knowledge or practice, they may misjudge creative behaviours or learning needs.

The second dimension in the model is teachers' optimism or pessimism. How teachers feel about their students' creativity is an important determinant for students' creative development in the future, as creativity may be accompanied by novelty, which many teachers do not feel comfortable with. When teachers have pessimistic feelings, their responses to signs of creativity, for example, asking frequent questions, independence, nonconformity to classroom rules and divergent thinking, might also be negative. When teachers have optimistic emotions, they respond positively to the same behaviours.

In fostering creative learning, sensitive teachers synthesise new and original products. They use existing resources such as educational materials, different power divisions in the society, economical resources and children's entry level characteristics, as well as their own teaching skills, such as optimism, a sense of humour, curiosity and creative problem solving skills. Teachers should evaluate each child's unique abilities separately and focus on designing their teaching styles and environments for each individual child's optimal benefit.

References

Aksoy, M (1996) *Eastern Anatolia in Cultural Sociology*. Istanbul: TISAV Publishers (Turkish)

Ayçiçeği A and Haris, C L (2003) When personality and culture clash: the psychological distress of allocentrics in an individualistic culture and idiocentrics in a collectivist culture. *Transcultural Psychiatry*

Bhargava,, R (1992) *Individualism in Social Science: forms and limits of a methodology*. Oxford: Clarendon Press

Bruell, C (1999) *On the Socratic Education: an introduction to the shorter Platonic dialogues.* Lanham, MD: Rowman and Littlefield

Carpenter, S and Karakitapoğlu-Aygün, Z (2005) Identity issues: how do the identities of Turkish women and men compare to those of American women and men? Paper presented at *Turkey at the Crossroads: Women, Women's Studies, and the State Symposium.* Istanbul: Turkey May 27

Celep, C and Bülbül, T (2003) *Öğretmenlerin okul dışına kendini adama odakları. eğitim ve bilim,* 28 (127) p37-44 (Teachers' Commitments to School and Non-School Institutions), *Education and Science*, 28, (127) p37-44)

Cohen, Anthony P (1985) *The Symbolic Construction of Community.* New York: Routledge

Dawkins, R (2000) Selfish Genes and Selfish *Memes.* In D R Hofstadter and D C Dennett (eds) *Mind's Eye.* New York: Basic Books Inc

Franzoi, S L (2000) *Social Psychology.* New York: McGraw-Hill

Gillingham, P (2006) Ambiguous missionaries: rural teachers and state facades in Guerrero. 1930-1950. *Mexican Studies-Estudios Mexicanos*, 22 (2) p331-360 Summer

Goncalo, J A, and Staw, B M (2006) Individualism, collectivism and group Creativity. *Organizational Behaviour and Human Decision Processes*, 100 (1) p96-109

Gordon, T (1999) Etkili Öğretmenlik Eğitimi, Istanbul: Sistem Yayıncılık (Efficient Teaching, Istanbul: Sistem Press)

Günçer, B. and Oral, G. (1993) Relationships between creativity and nonconformity to school discipline as perceived by teachers of Turkish elementary school children, by controlling for their grade and sex. *Journal of Instructional Psychology*, 20(3) p208-215 .

Jung, C (1970) *Psychic Conflicts in a Child: collected works of C G Jung.* USA: Princeton University Press

Kim, U (2001) Culture, science and indigenous psychologies: An integrated analysis In D Matsumoto (ed) *Handbook of Culture and Psychology.* Oxford: Oxford University Press

Kim, U, Triandis, H C, Kagitcibasi, C, Choi, S C and Yoon, G (eds) (1994) *Individualism and Collectivism: Theory, Method and Applications.* Newbury Park, CA: Sage

Marcus, H R, Kitayama, S and Heiman, R J (1996) Culture and 'basic' psychological principles. In E T Higgins and A W Kruglanski (eds) *Social Psychology: Handbook of Basic Principles* (p857-913). New York: Guilford Press

Marcus, H R and Kitayama, S (1991) Culture and the self: implications for cognition, emotion and motivation. *Psychological Review*, 98 p224-253

Masanori, N (1998) The history textbook controversy and nationalism. *Bulletin of Concerned Asian Scholars*, 30 (2) p24-29 Apr-Jun

Oral, G (2006) Collective unconscious in artistic creativity: the Anatolian case. Paper and poster Presented at the *52nd Annual International Creative Problem Solving Institute* June 24-30, Loyola University, Chicago

Shane, S A (1992) Why do some societies invent more than others? *Journal of Business Venturing*, 7 (1) p29-46

Shkedi, A and Horenczyk, G (1995) The role of teacher ideology in the teaching of culturally valued texts, *Teaching and Teacher Education* 11 (2) p107-117

Üskül, A K, Hynie, M and Lalonde, R N (2004) Interdependence as a mediator between culture and interpersonal closeness for Euro-Canadians and Turks. *Journal of Cross-Cultural Psychology*, 35 (2) p174-191

Whitmont, Edward C (1969) *The Symbolic Quest.* Princeton University Press

2

Creative learning:
definitions and barriers

David Spendlove and Dominic Wyse

The United Kingdom Department for Media, Culture and Sport (DCMS), then Department for Education and Skills (DfES)[1] and the Arts Council have funded the Creative Partnerships initiative since 2002. This has released £150 million to support the development of creative learning in over 1,000 primary and secondary schools, working with more than 550,000 young people, 50,000 teachers and over 4,500 creative practitioners in 36 areas of the country by 2007. Inspired by *All Our Futures,* the report from the National Advisory Committee on Creative and Cultural Education (NACCCE, 1999), the main aim of the initiative was to 'provide school children across England with the opportunity to develop creativity in learning and to take part in cultural activities of the highest quality' (Creative Partnerships, 2005a, para1).

Creative Partnerships originally defined creative learning as follows:

> Creative learning is simply any learning that develops our capacity to be creative. It equips young people with the knowledge and skills they need to succeed in today's world, nurturing ways of thinking and working that encourage imagination, independence, tolerance of ambiguity and risk, openness, the raising of aspirations. (Creative Partnerships, 2005b, para 2)

This chapter explores research and theory in the areas of creativity and creative learning in order to critique the creative partnerships definition shown above. A review of key literature in the field is supported by research carried out across two creative partnerships.

1 In July 2007, DfES was re-named the Department for Children, Schools and Families (DCSF).

Guilford's (1950) address to the American Psychological Association represented an early attempt to draw creativity and learning together. He stated that 'a creative act is an instance of learning... a comprehensive learning theory must take into account both insight and creative activity' (p446). Within this context a significant tension exists in recent work on creativity in England such as that carried out as part of Creative Partnerships, that has been related to early attempts to understand the differences between creativity, learning and creative learning. A recent manifestation of this is Banaji and Burn's (2006) review of the 'rhetorics of creativity'. Its Foreword includes the idea that 'Creative Partnerships in general espouses an eclectic notion of creativity. In a large and complex national programme, it does not pretend to simply follow one narrow use of the term' (p3). Although we agree with aspects of this statement, we believe that if research is to move forward and if Creative Partnerships is to have a lasting influence on practice there must be some clarity which includes a definition of creative learning that builds upon previous research in the field.

Drawing upon creativity research

Individual creativity can be affected by personality, reward and criticism (Berger and Ferguson, 1990), and by environmental stimuli, including time pressure, evaluation of work by others, fear of disturbing the *status quo* and political constraints (Amabile, 1988). Csikszentmihalyi (1990) proposed that creativity is not solely an individual attribute but also part of societal judgments involving interaction among a domain (opportunities and constraints), a person and a field (specialists) whilst Amabile (1996) focused on the notion of societal judgments by encouraging participants to create products which were rated by expert judges for evidence of creativity:

> A product or response is creative to the extent that appropriate observers independently agree it is creative. Appropriate observers are those familiar with the domain in which the product was created or the response articulated. (p33)

These promising lines of thinking fit well with Vernon's (1989) definition, which continues to be relevant:

> Creativity means a person's capacity to produce new or original ideas, insights, restructurings, inventions, or artistic objects, which are accepted by experts as being of scientific, aesthetic, social, or technological value. (p94)

However, the distinction between 'experts' and 'appropriate observers' is significant.

Vernon's definition is useful to current debates about creativity and learning because it offers a succinct way of thinking about creativity. When this defini-

12

tion is applied to possible acts of creativity through a process of consensual judgements, this offers a powerful tool for thinking about processes that could be called creative.

Although the origins of the definitions of creativity are predominantly drawn from the psychology research field, much of the research on creative learning has generally been developed within a socio-cultural research context. Consequently, some would question the validity of interchanging the terms creativity and creative learning. This prompts us to attempt to define creative learning.

Defining creative learning

Woods' (1995, p3) seminal work suggests that during creative learning 'pupils have control over their own learning processes, and ownership of the knowledge produced, which is relevant to their concerns'. According to Jeffrey and Craft (2004), relatively few studies have considered the student's role in the creative learning process but

> ...early findings have shown that students use their imagination and experience to develop their learning; they strategically collaborate over tasks; contribute to the classroom curriculum and pedagogy; and evaluate critically their own learning practices and teachers' performance. (p85)

Jeffrey and Craft (2004, p86) also emphasise the importance of the process of learning rather than the achievement of a creative output, artefact or interface. They believe that creative learning can be attained by 'focusing on the relationship between the creative teaching of the teacher and the creative learning of the learner'. As such, creative learning is conceived as the middle ground that emphasises the pedagogical processes involved in working creatively (Jeffrey and Craft, 2004).

Although the NACCCE report was well-received, ambiguous language resulted in the need for a much clearer focus on creative learning. An attempt to achieve this was evident in a leading edge seminar held in 2002 by the National College for School Leadership (NCSL). The role of the influential NCSL is to provide a single national focus for school leadership development through research and innovation, and the aim of the seminar was to reach a consensus on the term creative learning in the context of leading the creative school:

> ...there was a sense, for some, that creative learning was about the unfettered freedom of personal expression, a natural impulse to be celebrated, developed or often subdued by education. Other delegates, by contrast, emphasised the discipline, practice and craft of creativity progressively developed through learning. (NCSL, 2002, p2)

Demos, an independent think tank with influence on government thinking and Creative Partnerships, defined creative learning unsatisfactorily as 'finding ways to generate a new perspective on an existing question or practice, and therefore to understand it more deeply' (Bentley, 2002, p1). This definition fails to locate the concept of learning within a creative process and neither is there reference to the value of a 'new perspective'. More significantly, Demos also drew attention to the apparent tension between the creative learning envisaged by Creative Partnerships and what might be seen as old fashioned ideas about arts in schools, arguing that sustainability was a key requirement.

For the last couple of years researchers have been attempting to articulate a stable definition of creative learning, which is necessary for evaluating the extent to which work in schools is creative. Drawing upon previous creativity research and a study of 50 schools across two creative partnerships, Spendlove and Wyse (2005) put forward the following definition of creative learning,

> As Guilford (1950) argued, a creative act is an instance of learning, if so, we suggest that creative learning is a creative act. Therefore, creative learning is learning which leads to new or original thinking which is accepted by appropriate observers as being of value. (Spendlove and Wyse, 2005, p8)

In addition to locating this definition in relation to Guildford's work, we modified Vernon's (1989) influential definition and simplified Mackinnon's (1962) three key points of originality, adaptiveness and realisation. Our definition also accepted and built on the notion that creativity is something that is consensually assessed.

An International Symposium held at the University of Cambridge in 2005 drew upon growing research and interest in Creative Learning such as the European Creative Learning and Student Perspectives (CLASP) project and the Specialist Schools Trust creative learning and specialist subjects (CLASS) project. A conclusion from the conference was that

> one of the outcomes of our thinking about how we document creative learning, was a renewed focus on clarifying what it is we think we are capturing evidence about, and the urgent need for a flexible and evolutionary, and yet stable definition of 'creative learning'. (Craft, 2005, p5)

Since this symposium, the definition has evolved further. Our own latest iteration reads: 'creative learning develops our capacity for imaginative activity, leading to outcomes which are judged by appropriate observers to be original and of value' (Spendlove *et al*, 2005). The replacement of 'thinking' with 'outcomes' is significant and is discussed below. This latest definition has

14

been used to inform further research into creative learning, most notably the Creative Partnerships funded Progression in Creative Learning (PiCL) study (Craft *et al*, 2006), which led to a further definition recognising the development of knowledge:

> significant imaginative achievement as evidenced in the creation of new knowledge as determined by the imaginative insight of the person or persons responsible and judged by appropriate observers to be both original and of value as situated in different domain contexts. (*ibid*, p77)

This definition made explicit the consensual assessment embedded in our original definition (Spendlove and Wyse, 2005) and connected imagination with development of knowledge, together with the need to be able to evaluate some sort of outcome, or product.

Our own original definition stressed thinking, rather than products, as central; this was a reflection of the belief that all creative learning requires a distinct process of thought. There may or may not be a tangible product as an outcome. We recognise that it is difficult for appropriate observers to make a judgement that such creative thinking has taken place. The replacement of the term *thinking* with the word *outcomes* may be useful provided this helps in the evaluation of creative learning through creative artefacts or behavioural outcomes, such as being able to take risks and to deal with uncertainty.

The reason for reflecting on these distinctions is based on our concern about the danger of ignoring the creative process in pursuit of predictable products as outcomes. These practices can result in situations where ownership of the activity lies with the teacher, and the learner is relegated to making low level choices related to pre-determined options. In these situations, because the creative process is inherently risky, it becomes marginalised by the safe production of predictable rather than creative outcomes. These practices have become apparent in much of the performance-dominated school culture – which can represent a further barrier to creativity.

Barriers to creative learning

Craft (2005) suggested that fundamental limitations to the development of creativity in education relate to the 'technicisation' of teaching, the limitations of emerging terminologies, conflicts in policy and practice, and limitations stemming from centrally defined pedagogical practice. As part of research with two creative partnerships, we interviewed teachers, creative practitioners and school managers for their views on a range of issues, including what the barriers were to implementing creative learning. Following analysis of the data, three categories of barriers were prominent: statutory, organisational and pedagogical.

Barriers attributed to statutory requirements included statutory tests with an emphasis upon 'attainment rather than achievement', the national curriculum, the literacy and numeracy strategies, and the existence of an audit culture. A frequently highlighted constraint was the demands of Ofsted (Office for Standards in Education) school inspections, which have had a strong influence on school policy. There was a feeling that creativity was not sufficiently emphasised as part of the Ofsted inspection framework; as one headteacher noted 'they've got their eyes fixed on the plastic plates that are spinning and they take their eyes off ... the bone china ones'.

Organisational barriers were associated with competing demands that existed in schools. This meant that it was often difficult to arrange cross-faculty or department work in schools, particularly when support from headteachers or senior management teams was poor or inadequate. Another barrier, highlighted by some headteachers, was parental influence. Parents often had a clear view of what they expected from education but their views sometimes conflicted with the views of schools. This was exemplified by the suggestion that some parents felt 'that what you should be doing in schools is not prancing around the hall pretending that you're a Roman soldier'.

Pedagogical barriers included the concept of playing safe. Although teachers wanted to take risks, the effects of accountability were felt, particularly in terms of being accountable to children, to parents and to headteachers. A school senior manager said that he thought that teachers had become de-skilled: 'I think some people are so entrenched in a way of delivering the curriculum that they would feel very vulnerable [if] given too much freedom'; this meant that teachers were unable to model the attributes they were supposed to encourage. A further pedagogical barrier was revealed in the context of support from artists and other creative practitioners. Although their contributions were valued, the creative practitioners sometimes lacked knowledge about children's development, appropriate pedagogy and issues such as school health and safety practice. When listening to both artists' and teachers' observations, it was apparent that both sides were capable of magnifying these tensions, and that their resolution would mean stronger partnerships which could benefit all concerned.

Recommendations for future policy and planning

Since defining creativity has been an issue for many years, early attempts to define creative learning have generated much debate. This debate is necessary for the creative learning research to move forward and for Creative Partnerships to have a lasting influence on practice.

Within the significant body of research in the creativity field, a much smaller body of research has looked at the way that creative learning is defined and understood. If creative learning is defined predominantly as in terms of different teaching or learning styles, how will the impact of Creative Partnerships differ from countless other initiatives that have attempted to change teacher practice? The word 'creative' should be distinct, reflecting something genuinely different rather than a mere change in teacher practice, although teaching will need to change if creative learning of whatever definition is to take place.

One of the limitations of our data about participants' perceptions of barriers to creative learning is that it was collected without an agreed definition for creative learning. Perceived barriers were therefore contextualised in personal, not shared, understanding. The two most significant barriers identified were the assessment system and the formal curriculum. The national literacy and numeracy strategies, which are part of the formal curriculum, were considered a particularly strong barrier to creative learning.

Amidst much uncertainty, there was an overriding feeling that creative learning represented something less formal, less restrictive and more creative than previous practice. These feelings can be regarded as a backlash to the stifling effects of an accountability culture that has pervaded the English education system and led to the technicisation of teaching. Unsurprisingly, the opportunity for teachers to recapture the curriculum and promote pupil autonomy through an attempt to stimulate creative learning opportunities has been fundamental to Creative Partnerships activities. Inevitably, the aspiration to move to a more desirable state while still inculcated within the straightjacket of the prevailing accountability culture has proved troublesome for many participants. Many of their efforts, albeit considerable, have been nullified.

Since the inception of Creative Partnerships, the creativity field in England has re-engaged with debates that were a feature of the discourse in many countries during the earlier part of the 20th century. Recent work reminds us that definitions of creativity are culturally and socially bound, mediated as part of a shifting cultural capital (Craft, 2005) by the cultures from which they emerge.

17

The perception within such a context, that attempting to define creativity, or creative learning satisfactorily is not possible because of its eclectic nature or because post-modern rhetoric render this undesirable, does not seem appropriate. Judgements about whether children's creativity or creative learning have been developed, or not, are significant in terms of evaluating the effectiveness of large scale programmes such as Creative Partnerships.

We are grateful to Creative Partnerships for funding to carry out the research.

References

Amabile, T M (1988) A model of creativity and innovation in organizations Research in *Organizational Behaviour* 10 p123-167

Amabile, T M (1996) *Creativity in Context.* Boulder, CO: Westview Press

Banaji, S and Burn, A (2006) *The Rhetorics of Creativity: A review of the literature.* London: Arts Council England

Bentley, T (2002) *Distributed Intelligence: leadership, learning and creativity.* National College for School Leadership Leading Edge Seminar, Nottingham, 22 November 2002

Berger, F and Ferguson, D H (1990) *Innovation: Creativity techniques for hospitality managers.* New York: Wiley and Sons

Craft, A (2005) *Creativity in Schools: Tensions and Dilemmas.* Oxford: Routledge Falmer

Craft, A, Grainger, T, Burnard, P, and Chappell, K (2006) *Progression in Creative Learning* (PICL Pilot): A study funded by Creative Partnerships. http://www.creative-partnerships.com/content/researchAndEvaluationProjects/139847/?version=1 (May 2007)

Creative Partnerships (2005a) Creative Partnership Website. http://www.creative-partnerships.com/aboutcp (February 2005)

Creative Partnerships (2005b) Creative Partnership Website. http://www.creative-partnerships.com/cpandyou/creatives (February 2005)

Csikszentmihalyi, M (1990) The Domain of Creativity, in M Runco and R Albert (eds), *Theories of Creativity.* London: Sage, p190-212

Guilford, J P (1950) Creativity. *American Psychologist* 5 p444-454

Jeffrey, B and Craft, A (2004) Teaching creatively and teaching for creativity: distinctions and relationships. *Educational Studies* 30(1) p77-87

MacKinnon, D W (1962) The nature and nurture of creative talent. *American Psychologist* 17 p484-495

National Advisory Committee On Creative And Cultural Education (NACCCE) (1999) *All Our Futures: Creativity, Culture and Education.* London: Department for Education and Employment

National College of School Leadership (2002) *Leading the Creative School: a Leading Edge Seminar,* Nottingham – November 2002

Spendlove, D and Wyse, D (2005) Definitions and barriers: teachers' perceptions of creative learning. Paper presented at *Documenting Creative Learning Symposium: What, How and Why?* University of Cambridge, April 2005

Spendlove, D, Wyse, D, Craft, A, Hallgarten, J (2005) *Creative Learning Definition: work in progress* – private correspondence emerging from Documenting Creative Learning International Symposium held at University of Cambridge, April 2005

Vernon, P (1989) The nature-nurture problem in creativity, in J Glover, R Ronning and C Reynolds (eds) *Handbook of creativity.* London: Plenum Press, 93-98

Woods, P (1995) *Creative teachers in primary schools.* Buckingham: Open University Press

3

Creative learning and new pedagogies in China

Keang Ieng [Peggy] Vong

From political interest to national guidelines

Several announcements made by international bodies at the outset of this new millennium were particularly important for the People's Republic of China. Among them was the World Trade Organisation's acceptance of China as one of its members. Although China's economic growth has accelerated continuously over the past 30 years, making her a rising power in the world, competition with other nations has also escalated.

In China's eleventh Five-Year Plan, announced in March 2006, the significance of fostering creativity or training children to be creative individuals, who are innovative and can come up with new ideas and products in their line of work, became a priority. In the Western world, creativity has been studied widely. Early years programmes that emphasise the role of creativity in the curriculum are found in Western educational settings (Jeffrey and Woods, 2003; Craft, 2000; Duffy, 1998). However, the significance of fostering creativity in Chinese educational settings has not received much attention until recent years.

At present, 'foster creativity in children' is one of the most commonly used slogans in Chinese kindergartens. Its meaning is spelt out in the arts section of the latest national Guidelines for Early Childhood Education – Trial Version (*Early Childhood Education*, 2001). In this document, the importance of encouraging young children to be creative and expressive and to respect independent thinking is highlighted, as well as the need to avoid training for skills and memorising of knowledge only.

The document advocates a relatively children-centred educational ideology which necessitates a child-centred pedagogy and is supported by the majority of western educators. Nonetheless, the notion of creativity as understood by Chinese teachers, and the strategies through which creativity is fostered in a culture which is different from the Western one, deserves thorough investigation. Teaching is not independent of learning. Moreover, for the study of creative pedagogies, the concepts of teaching creatively and creative learning should be distinguished (Jeffrey and Craft, 2004). Whether children can be fostered as creative individuals by means of teaching strategies is related to the kind of learning opportunities that they are given.

This chapter begins by presenting different views of learning. These are followed by some Chinese practitioners' interpretations of learning and creativity. Next, examples are given of a 'new' pedagogy which aims at promoting creativity. In conclusion, the relationship is outlined between learning, creative learning and a new pedagogy developed to foster creativity in Chinese children.

Perspectives on learning

Even though China was once famous for her discoveries, the ability to create did not gain enough attention and the amount of literature which documents ancient Chinese creation in relation to fostering creativity is scanty. As recently as 1930, eminent Chinese scholars such as Heqin Chen and XingzhiTao, who had studied in the US under Dewey, drew people's attention to the importance of fostering creativity in children (He, 1988). Wang, Qiang and Huang (1998) describe how, in the 1990s, Chinese scholars translated Western theories and studies about creativity and there were increasingly more studies on creativity at different levels. Teaching, no matter how creative, is always complemented by learning so that there is a need to examine the different perspectives of learning.

In a Chinese translation of the book *Creativity in the Classroom: Schools of Curious Delight* (Liu and Ceng, 2003), learning is explained in terms of the constructivist viewpoints – that learners actively construct their knowledge system rather than passively absorbing knowledge. The book highlights the core concept that teaching for creativity should focus on the learner rather than on the teacher's strategies. These views are rooted in western ideas of learning and creativity.

Heqin Chen stressed that early childhood education should be suited to the special circumstances of mainland China (He, 1988). He quoted Heqin Chen's views on the teaching and learning of arts

...pictures should be drawn by one self, but it takes guidance. If a child draws by himself casually, without teachers' guidance, he cannot draw good pictures... But how to guide them, I have several methods: one is by demonstration, one is by correction... (He, 1988, p84)

Based on classroom observations during his visit to China, Gardner (1989) stated that Chinese children's drawings could be creative even though the teachers' strategies were full of demonstrations and direct instructions.

In a book written for teacher training programmes, Pan (1993) drew on Karl Marx's theories. He stressed the importance of seeing the child as the 'main or primary figure' in learning and of stimulating the child's awareness of their role in the teaching and learning process. Pan clarified that teachers should still be in the directive position during the process. According to Pan, the underlying meaning of the 'main figure' in the teaching and learning process is that the child's active participation, initiative and interests, should be considered carefully by teachers when designing teaching activities.

Wu (1993) emphasised the skills and techniques involved in art work by explaining that '...without mastering the lines, shades, use of colours, and other key knowledge about drawing; without witnessing how others draw; there is no way to master the skills in drawing...' (p108). Wu reminded teachers that providing children with basic knowledge and skills are equally important in early years' learning.

Research work supported by the tenth Five-Year Plan in China has generated local theories on creative learning and how to foster such ability in elementary and secondary school students (Ye, Lu, Ke and Zhu, 2004). According to this line of research,

Learning means behavioural changes that are resulted from interactions between the main figure and other objects. These interactions are internalised and become experiences and externalised as behavioural changes. (*ibid*, 2004, p2)

According to these researchers, creative learning is a learning style which requires students to incorporate reality, independent thinking, combination processing, bold exploration, new ideas and methods, all with the guidance of teachers (*ibid*, p5). Following this principle, teachers are expected to play the role of facilitators while children are seen as the main figures in the learning process. The researchers add that creative learning is not independent of foundational knowledge which has to be passed on from teachers to learners. However, learners should be aware that while they are inheriting knowledge and experiences of the past, they cannot just absorb what is given to them:

they must select, even change, the knowledge inherited in order to adapt to the need of new situations (*ibid*, p 4-5).

According to these perspectives, the teacher's role in the process of teaching and learning should change from a directive role to a facilitating role. The discussion reveals a recent perspective of learning and creative learning. In practice, there is now a need to foster creativity in children. What are the Chinese teachers' interpretations of learning and creativity? Does the new pedagogy focus on teaching creatively on the teachers' part or allowing for creative learning on the children's part? Either way, how does it happen? A study conducted in a Chinese city called Zhuhai SER, which is situated in the southern part of China, examined some Chinese practitioners' views of learning and creativity, as well as the new pedagogy that they have recently developed to foster creativity in children.

Background to the study

The public kindergarten in this study is a subsidiary of the Customs Department in Zhuhai SER and is called Customs Kindergarten. Since the Guidelines for early childhood education advocate teaching for creativity (*Early Childhood Education*, 2001), kindergartens in mainland China are keen to modify their curricula to meet the expectations of the central government. Many experimented with working through projects. This western pedagogy is based on progressive educational ideas that advocate liberal teaching styles and play-based activities. Since art work activities such as junk-modelling are prominent features of a project-based approach, and are generally considered an effective way to allow children create and imagine, Customs Kindergarten expected that by adapting to art activities similar to those featured in a project approach, children's creativity could be fostered.

The study

The study aimed at understanding the Chinese practitioners' interpretations of learning and creativity as well as the new pedagogy they employ to foster creativity in children. Data were collected within an ethnographic framework and by means of participant observation, semi-structured interviews, a daily journal, visual data such as video-recordings and photos, and documentation of worksheets, exercise books and notes for parents.

As a researcher and teacher trainer sharing the participants' Chinese culture and larger working environment, I spent two days of each week over a four-month period in 2001 at two 5 and 6 year-olds' classrooms at Customs Kindergarten in Zhuhai SER and at those in its neighbouring city, although only the findings from Customs Kindergarten are presented here. The Chinese teachers at Customs Kindergarten were invited to watch edited clips of visual data and comment on the creativity and educational value of their new teaching pedagogy in terms of children's creativity and learning.

Zhuhai SER kindergarten teachers' views of learning and creativity

According to the Zhuhai SER, teachers' comments on the visual data not only reveal what they think learning is but also what learning meant in the past. Evidence shows that the meaning of the term 'learning' has changed over time; there is a tendency to pay attention to the learner as an active individual and to the process of learning rather to its result.

> Head teacher: In the traditional concept, learning means he imitates what I say, that's learning, teachers teach, children learn, all is about imitation... I draw a picture and you draw one that's exactly the same,... now, it's about innovation, breaking the restrictions of Chinese education, advocate creativeness, or children innovate... now learning is about independence, creativeness and autonomy.

However, there is still a strong belief among the teachers that imitation is a means to learn and practise is considered a key factor in learning.

> Art teacher: xue xi (Chinese term for learning) can be interpreted separately... xue is to follow what the teacher does and xi is to practise, the process of repeatedly practise until skilful.

> Science teacher: Following others is a kind of learning.

These practitioners' ideas of learning, which emphasise imitation and practise, are similar to the views stated by Chinese scholars, such as Chen, Tao, Pan and Wu mentioned earlier. Nonetheless, the head teacher pointed out that learning is about the learner's initiative in the process and this reflects one of the latest views of creative learning (Ye *et al*, 2004). The implication may be that the understanding of learning is still disparate among practitioners.

There is a general consensus among teachers that creativity could not possibly take place without foundational knowledge and skills. More specifically, children should base their initial learning on what teachers have mentioned in a lesson and then, when given free rein by the teachers, they should develop the basic information further into their own thinking and ideas. One of the class teachers explained that 'It's an ability to innovate... the process of absorbing knowledge and then accepting it, then apply to innovation.' Another class teacher added,

My initial understanding of creativity was that it was something of one's free desire... being away from normal reasoning was creativity, being in strange forms was creativity ... but after working for a long time, I feel that there must be a very strong skill in it ... and a solid foundation in it before you can let go your imagination and then tell others how you create this thing with theories and evidence...

The class teacher's comments reveal that, despite her initial understanding of theories of creativity, her teaching experiences have informed her of the need to build up children's foundational knowledge and skills if creative ideas are to emerge.

A new pedagogy document – an example

These Chinese teachers' understanding of learning and creativity are made manifest in their new pedagogy. The following transcribed recordings exemplify the pedagogical strategies that the teachers at Customs kindergarten employed to conduct their art work lessons. Children were expected to make animals with foam board pieces that teachers had prepared for them. When the whole group was seated, the class teacher stood in front of the class and demonstrated how to join the pieces of foam board together by inserting toothpicks as joints to make the different parts of an animal.

Teacher: How about this? Do you think it looks like an elephant? If you don't think so, you can use a shorter piece to make the nose. And then, what else, we can make a big and fat, what?

Children: Body.

Teacher: Yes (while she adds a square piece below the round one to make a body and then looks for two short rectangular pieces to be the front leg and the hind leg).

Teacher: When you find the leg and what?

Children: Hand.

Teacher: Hand. Both are possible. You join them to the body and you will turn it into, what?

Children: An elephant.

Teacher: An elephant, but it's just one side. There is another side (while she continues to finish the attachments).

When the constructed elephant was completed (see photograph opposite), the teacher showed her product to the class and told them that they could make other animals or objects.

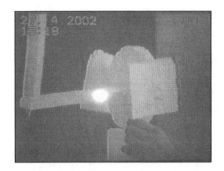

Teacher shows children her finished work

Discussion and implications

This study reveals that there are cultural characteristics to learning and creativity. Findings show that for Chinese scholars and practitioners, learning is fundamentally associated with their teachers' direction and guidance, in the form of direct instructions and demonstrations, and children's imitations of ideas provided by teachers. Creativity could not have happened prior to an accumulation of foundational knowledge and skills. Practitioners strongly believe that when learners are given opportunities to apply the information acquired, innovation and creative thinking will occur. Taken together, the role of Chinese teachers in the process of learning and the teaching strategies to foster creativity in children are crucial. Despite the suggestion that the teachers' role could change from a directive position where teachers design and instruct activities to a guiding position where children actively incorporate knowledge and skills under guidance, for these practitioners learning and creativity are impossible unless the teachers give step-by-step induction of knowledge and ideas.

This study also reveals that the new pedagogy is still essentially teacher-directed, so that teaching creatively is still the main focus of the pedagogy. Since the role of teachers is so important in children's learning in the Chinese context studied, creative learning opportunities are seen to come only after the teachers' teaching strategies have been made clear. The teachers' creative pedagogy is a springboard from which children's creative ideas can take off. When assessing the amount of creative learning opportunities for Chinese pupils, such as freedom and initiation, the nature of teaching and learning in Chinese classrooms should be taken into account.

Conclusion

In the current national guidelines for kindergarten education, teachers are expected to teach creatively and create an environment for children to initiate learning. However, in the Chinese educational arena, indigenous ideas of education are still in place. Even though children are gradually coming to be seen as the main figure in the teaching and learning process, the teacher's guiding role is still seen as a critical stage in the fostering of creativity in children. Imitation is regarded as the necessary initial stage before children's creativity can be manifest. For these reasons, new pedagogies in China should be understood in terms of the cultural characteristics inherent in China's specific social context.

References

Craft, A (2000) *Creativity Across the Primary Curriculum: Framing and Developing Practice.* London: Routledge

Duffy, B (1998) *Supporting Creativity and Imagination in the Early Years.* Buckingham: Open University Press

Early Childhood Education (2001) (in Chinese) The Guidelines for Early Childhood Education – Trial Version. September p4-5

Gardner, H (1989) *To Open Minds.* New York: Basic Books

He, Xiao Xia (1988) (in Chinese) Xingzhi Tao's Thoughts and Implementation of Early Childhood Education. *Preschool Education- Materials for Distance Learning.* p92-99

Jeffrey, B and Craft, A (2004) Teaching creatively and teaching for creativity: distinctions and relationships. *Educational Studies* 30 (1) p77-87

Jeffrey, B and Woods, P (2003) *The Creative School: A Framework for Success, Quality and Effectiveness.* London: Routledge Falmer

Liu, X L and Ceng, S C (2003) (Trans) *Creativity in the Classroom: Schools of Curious Delight.* 2nd Edition. Shanghai: East China Normal University Press

Pan, Jie (1993) (in Chinese) *The Foundations of Education for Early Childhood Education Teachers.* Henan: Henan Education Publishing House

Wang, H Z Gu, G Q and Huang, W H (1998) (in Chinese) *Creativity and the Development of Teaching Process.* Shanghai: Tong Ji University Press

Wu, C G (1993) (in Chinese) *The Psychology of Teaching.* Quangdong: Guangdong Education Publishing House

Ye, R, Lu, C N, Ke, B J and Zhu, S L (2004) (eds) (in Chinese) *Theories on creative learning abilities.* Tianjin: Tianjin Education Publishing House

4

The role of domains in creative learning in the USA

James Kaufman and John Baer

How people understand creative learning is evolving, and the use of this term has not yet been widely adopted in the US. The more common expressions in the US are creativity training, creativity enhancement and teaching for creativity. According to Craft *et al* (2006), although there is at present 'a lack of shared discourse concerning its nature and significance,' the term creative learning nonetheless implies 'a constructivist model of learning as meaning-making in a social context' with an 'emphasis on relevance, innovation, control and ownership, in creative teaching and learning'. These authors quote a definition by Spendlove *et al* (2005): 'creative learning develops our capacity for imaginative activity, leading to outcomes which are judged by appropriate observers to be original and of value' (p8-9).

This definition closely matches what is variously called in the US creativity training, creativity enhancement, or teaching for creativity. Among those who emphasise creative learning in the US and consistent with the conceptualisations of creative learning cited above, there is a growing sense that creative learning is congruent with a constructivist understanding of learning. There is also increasing recognition which teaching that values creativity in both teacher and student and that has the goal of increasing student creativity is also likely to benefit students by simultaneously promoting other kinds of learning, including the acquisition of content knowledge (Baer, 1997, 2002).

Teaching students to be more creative thinkers is an important part of the general educational programme in many US elementary schools, which educate students between the ages of 5 and 12 years. In schools where direct instruction in the area of creativity enhancement is offered, almost all such instruction focuses on teaching and practicing divergent thinking skills. This is true of both classroom-based instruction and extra-curricular creativity training programmes such as Odyssey of the Mind, a team competition in creative problem-solving that is popular, often as an after-school activity, in many schools. Tests of divergent thinking are also commonly used along with intelligence and achievement tests and teacher recommendations, in the selection process for special programmes for intellectually gifted and creatively talented students.

Evaluations of programmes designed to improve divergent thinking skills have demonstrated considerable success both at raising scores on divergent thinking tests, which is how improvements in creative-thinking skills are most commonly documented; and also success at enhancing creative performance on assessments that go beyond divergent thinking testing to evaluate more real-world creative performance – although the results are far more robust for the former claim (Baer, 1993). Rose and Lin (1984) undertook a comprehensive meta-analysis of the long-term effects of creativity training programmes that focused on divergent thinking. These were primarily studies of elementary school-aged children, but among the 46 programmes included in their study there were a few that focused on adolescents and adults.

Their analysis yielded an average overall effect size of .468. Effect size is to measure the magnitude of a treatment effect. It is used to provide a uniform way of comparing the impact of any experimental treatment. An effect size of .2 is considered small, .5 medium, and .8 large. Among the group of programmes in this analysis that had the most consistent effect – those using the Osborn-Parnes CPS programme (Parnes and Noller, 1973) – an impressive average effect size of .629 was found for the eight studies in which this training programme was used. All the studies in the Rose and Lin meta-analysis have been criticised, however, because the training exercises and test questions were similar and from the same domains, providing little evidence of either real-world creative performance or transferability to tasks unlike those used in the training and testing (Baer, 1993).

The most common activity used in elementary school programmes aimed at increasing creativity is brainstorming, as in 'List as many different possible uses for empty egg cartons as you can' or 'In what ways might one convince one's parents to buy an iguana for a household pet?'. The rules of brainstorming are fairly simple:

* defer judgment

* avoid ownership of ideas. When people feel that an idea is theirs, egos sometimes get in the way of creative thinking. They are likely to be more defensive later when ideas are critiqued, and they are less willing to allow their ideas to be modified

* feel free to hitchhike on other ideas. This means that it's okay to borrow elements from ideas already on the table, or to make slight modifications of ideas already suggested

* wild ideas are encouraged. Impossible, totally unworkable ideas may lead someone to think of other, more possible, more workable ideas. It's easier to take a wildly imaginative bad idea and tone it down to fit the constraints of reality than to take a boring bad idea and make it interesting enough to be worth thinking about. (Baer, 1997, p. 43)

Other programmes designed to enhance creativity that are popular in elementary schools include Synectics (Gordon, 1961), Talents Unlimited (2006), CPS (Eberle and Stanish, 1980), and the Odyssey of the Mind (formerly known as the Olympics of the Mind; Micklus, 1986; Micklus and Micklus, 1986). In all these programmes the development of divergent thinking skill is paramount and brainstorming is employed as a primary tool for encouraging and improving divergent thinking.

In recent years, a serious challenge to many creativity development programmes has come from claims that creative thinking is domain specific (Baer, 1993, 1998; Gardner, 1983, 1998; Kaufman and Baer, 2004a, 2004b, 2005a; Runco, 1987). Evidence from a variety of sources suggests that for both children and adults, creativity is very domain specific. Being creative in one domain, such as writing poetry, is not at all predictive of creativity in other domains, such as making collages (with correlations of creativity ratings hovering around zero).

There is also evidence that creativity-enhancement activities in a single domain lead to increased creative performance, but only in that one domain (Baer, 1993).

This evidence includes measurements of real-world creative performance across a variety of task domains, such as writing poetry, making collages, creating mathematical word problems, and writing and telling stories; self-report evidence in which children and adults are surveyed about the different areas in which they believe they are creative; and experimental studies of children's creativity in which students receive different kinds of creativity training and the impact on creative performance is been measured at a later date.

Because most creative learning activities in elementary school programmes have made an implicit assumption that creativity is a general cognitive skill easily transferable across domains, teachers have unfortunately not been concerned about the kinds of tasks they have used. Most if not all of these activities have tended to be of the same sort, such as divergent-thinking exercises in which children are encouraged to invent unusual uses for common objects. This can lead to two possible problems. At an immediate level, investment in these programmes may lead to an increase in creative-thinking abilities only in those domains, at the expense of other, less-obvious domains. In the long term, however, these activities may affect the self-esteem of children who are not creative in these select domains. Such children may decide that they are not creative, even though they may be creative in domains which have not been emphasised (Baer, 1993, 1997).

It is far better for teachers to provide a wide variety of divergent-thinking exercises. For example:

- asking young children to name as many words as they can that begin with a specific phoneme, such as 'How many words can we find that start with the 'f' sound, as in 'friend' and 'fire'?'

- giving children papers with a dozen circles on them and asking the them to turn each circle into something else

- at the beginning of a unit, getting children to make a list of everything they know about that topic

These kinds of activities allow children to exercise their divergent-thinking muscles in a wide variety of areas, and also allow the teacher to meet several other goals at the same time. In the first example above, children are not only practicing divergent thinking with sounds. They are also developing phonemic awareness, an important skill that children who are learning to read need as they learn to decode texts. Giving them the chance to recall everything they know about a topic about to be studied, as in the third example above, simultaneously allows the teacher to assess children's prior knowledge and misunderstandings of a topic, and to help activate children's prior knowledge. Connecting what they are about to learn with what they already know, makes the learning more meaningful and long-lasting. All this is in addition to the practice the children are getting in divergent thinking.

There is still considerable disagreement among creativity researchers and theorists about how domain specific creativity may be. In the only pair of point-counterpoint feature articles in its history, the *Creativity Research Journal* focused on this question a few years ago (Baer, 1998; Plucker, 1998). There is evidence to support both positions, and the likely answer is that there is truth in both the domain specificity and domain generality claims. But until this question is fully resolved, it is suggested that teachers assume that creative thinking skills, like divergent thinking, are *extremely* domain specific. If creativity is domain-general, then it doesn't matter at all what kinds of exercises are used, as any exercise that improves creative thinking will improve it equally in all domains. But if the domain specificity hypothesis is correct and a teacher assumes that divergent thinking skills on one task will transfer to any other creativity-relevant task, then much of her efforts to improve her pupils' divergent thinking skills may be wasted. She may be increasing creativity on only a very narrow range of activities, which are in the same domain as the exercises and having no impact at all on creativity in other areas (Baer, 1997).

To fill the need for a theory that accounts for both domain-general and domain-specific aspects of creativity, we proposed the APT, or Amusement Park Theory, model (Baer and Kaufman, 2005; Kaufman and Baer, 2005b, 2005c). This model uses the metaphor of an amusement park to explore creativity. First there are initial requirements of intelligence, motivation and environment, that must be present at some level for all creative work, just as there are certain basic requirements needed for admission to any amusements park, such as money to purchase a ticket and a means of transportation to get to the park.

Next, there are general thematic areas in which someone could be creative such as the arts or science. This level is the equivalent of deciding which type of amusement park to visit. The next level focuses on more specific domains within the general thematic area of the arts, could be such varied domains as writing, music and art. Similarly, once you have selected the type of amusement park you want to visit, you must choose a particular park. Finally, once you have settled on a domain, there are micro domains representing specific tasks associated with each domain, just as there are many individual rides to choose from once you are at an amusement park. In the domain of writing, there are the micro domains of poetry, short stories, drama and essays, etc.

This model attempts to integrate both general and domain-specific views of creativity. The first level of initial requirements is general. Each subsequent level gets more domain-specific. By the final level of micro domains, the theory is clearly domain-specific. Using the APT model, a teacher can target the kinds of creativity she wishes to enhance. For example, if a teacher's goal is to enhance creativity in a narrow domain, such as poetry-writing, she must choose exercises only from that domain. If the goal is wider, such as enhancing writing creativity more generally, she should choose exercises from a broad range of micro domains within the domain of writing. Casting a still wider net, targeting the general thematic area of the arts means using activities from many domains within that general thematic area. And to improve creative thinking skills even more generally means creating activities that come from all of the general thematic areas.

Education in the US is decentralised, each of the 50 states setting its own standards and goals. Even within states, local districts have a great deal of autonomy, especially about such things as creativity enhancement. The kinds of activities described above, such as brainstorming, Synectics, Odyssey of the Mind, CPS, and Talents Unlimited, as well as many similar programmes are actively pursued in some US schools, and hardly at all in others. It is all too easy for creativity to get lost in a standard-focused educational system. It is therefore even more important that those schools that emphasise creativity do so in ways that enable every student to be creative.

References

Baer, J (1993) *Creativity and divergent thinking: A task-specific approach*. Hillsdale, NJ: Lawrence Erlbaum Associates

Baer, J (1997) *Creative Teachers, Creative Students*. Boston: Allyn and Bacon

Baer, J (1998) The case for domain specificity in creativity. *Creativity Research Journal* 11 p173-177

Baer, J (2002) Are creativity and content standards allies or enemies? *Research in the Schools,* 9(2) p35-42

Baer, J, and Kaufman, J C (2005) Bridging generality and specificity: the amusement park theoretical (APT) model of creativity. *Roeper Review,* 27 p158-163

Craft, A, Burnard, T, Grainger, T and Chappell, K (2006) *Progression in creative learning*. Retrieved February 21, 2007, from University of Cambridge School of Education Web site: http://www.creative-partnerships.com/content/researchAndEvaluationProjects/139847/?version=1

Eberle, B and Stanish, B (1980) *CPS for kids: A resource book for teaching creative problem-solving to children*. Buffalo, NY: D.O.K. Publishers

Gardner, H (1983) *Frames of mind: The theory of multiple intelligences*. New York: Basic Books

Gardner, H (1988) Creative lives and creative works: A synthetic scientific approach. In R J Sternberg (ed), *The nature of creativity* (p298-321) Cambridge University Press

Gordon, W J J (1961) *Synectics*. New York: Harper and Row

Kaufman, J C and Baer, J (2004a) Hawking's haiku, Madonna's math: Why it's hard to be creative in every room of the house. In R J Sternberg, E L Grigorenko, and J L Singer (eds) *Creativity: from potential to realisation* (p3-19). Washington, DC: American Psychological Association

Kaufman, J C and Baer, J (2004b) Sure, I'm creative – but not in math!: Self-reported creativity in diverse domains. *Empirical Studies of the Arts,* 22(2) p143-155

Kaufman, J C and Baer, J (eds) (2005a) *Faces of the muse: How people think, work, and act creatively in diverse domains.* Hillsdale, NJ: Lawrence Erlbaum Associates

Kaufman, J C and Baer, J (2005b) How people think, work, and act creatively in diverse domains. In J C Kaufman and J Baer (eds), *Creativity across domains: Faces of the muse* (pp. xiii-xvii). Hillsdale, NJ: Lawrence Erlbaum Associates

Kaufman, J C and Baer, J (2005c) The amusement park theory of creativity. In J C Kaufman and J Baer (eds.), *Creativity across domains: Faces of the muse* (pp. 321-328). Hillsdale, NJ: Lawrence Erlbaum Associates

Micklus, C S (1986) *OM-AHA!: Problems to develop creative thinking skills.* Glassboro, NJ: Creative Competitions

Micklus, C S, and Micklus, C (1986) *OM programme handbook.* Glassboro, NJ: Creative Competitions

Parnes, S J and Noller, R B (1973) *Toward supersanity.* Buffalo, NY: D. O. K. Publishers

Plucker, J A (1998) Beware of simple conclusions: The case for the content generality of creativity. *Creativity Research Journal* 11, p179-182

Rose, L H and Lin, H (1984) A meta-analysis of long-term creativity training programmes. *Journal of Creative Behavior* 18 p11-22

Runco, M A (1987) The generality of creative performance in gifted and nongifted children. *Gifted Child Quarterly* 31 p121-125

Spendlove, D, Wyse, D, Craft, A and Hallgarten, J (2005) Creative Learning. Unpublished working document, May 2005

Talents Unlimited, Inc (2006) *Talents Unlimited.* Retrieved November 24, 2006, from the Talents Unlimited, Inc website: http://www.mcpss.com/websites/MCPSS/MCPSS/Default.asp?PN=Pages Level1&L=0andDivisionID='23'&DepartmentID='95'&SubDepartmentID="&PageID='510'

5

Creative learning in Europe: making use of global discourses

Bob Jeffrey

Interest and activity are increasing in the area of comparative cross-national partnership research (Troman and Jeffrey, 2005). This has been stimulated by methodological, ideological, political and economic developments, particularly within the European Union, where European Commission funding has supported numerous projects. While the old comparative education focused solely on large-scale quantitative projects to establish differences in the educational effectiveness of different nations, the new comparative research is developing innovative methodologies which take into account the tradition, context and national and local education policy of a study (Broadfoot, 2000, 2002b; Osborn, 2004).

More specifically the new research seeks to:

- understand, through cross-cultural comparison, the relationship between national context, institutional ethos and classroom practices in mediating the development of a learner's identity (Osborn, 2004, p.266)

- 'make the familiar strange in different national contexts' (Broadfoot, 2002a, p 6)

- examine the assumptions embedded in conventional discourses, through the use of systematic explanations of similar phenomena in different cultural, geographic, social and chronological settings (*ibid*). This approach is needed in order to provide knowledge through which academics, politicians and policy makers can under-stand the 'impact of economic and political pressures which make it difficult for countries to develop genuinely novel educational ap-proaches' (*ibid*).

Following this new path, the Creative Learning and Student Perspectives (CLASP) research project gained funding from the European Union to carry out international research into creative learning. This is an area in which there has been a 'neglect of pedagogy in comparative education' (Alexander, 2001, p 509) and CLASP's research supported the need to place much greater emphasis 'on the process of learning itself rather than at present, on the organisation and provision of education' (Broadfoot, 2000, p368). CLASP (Jeffrey, 2005; Jeffrey, 2006) was funded by the European Commission, with the UK element also part-funded by the ESRC (RES 000-22-0037). In this chapter only the research of the five CLASP project partners who focused on primary or elementary education is discussed.

Partners

Partner and principal researcher	Research sites
University of Innsbruck, Austria Andrea Raggl	One secondary and two primary classrooms in separate schools
The Open University, Milton Keynes, England Bob Jeffrey	Two primary schools and two primary dance projects
St Patrick's College, Dublin City University, Ireland Dr Ciaran Sugrue	Two primary classrooms and one special needs class
University of Strathclyde, Glasgow, Scotland Dr Geri Smyth	One primary school with a specialist bilingual unit
University of Cadiz, Spain Dr Ramon Porras Vallinjas	One Early Years school, one primary class and one secondary class

Figure 5.1: CLASP Research partners, principle researchers and research sites.

Policy background

According to the partner reports, new national discourses and policies relat-ing directly to creative and more flexible curriculum programmes have been introduced over the last few years in England, Ireland and Scotland. These have varied in extent, influence and character. England has extensively incor-porated creativity criteria across its national curriculum programmes and funded a national programme of arts and education projects. Ireland has renewed its commitment to child-centred education and focused on achievement levels, while Social, Personal and Health Education has been added to the curriculum and Drama has been elevated from a good pedagogical vehicle for learning to the status of a subject in its own right.

In Scotland, the New National Priorities include the encouragement of creativity and ambition. The attempt to incorporate some of the new policies has created tensions for schools and teachers, which were in conflict with contemporary policies and practices. Responses to the national and local reform of education ranged from evidence of teacher excitement, to uncertainty, anxiety, loss of professional autonomy and re-professionalisation, eg extending their management skills to cope with the implementation of new policies.

In Austria and Spain, although we found no evidence of the types of programmes in place in England, Ireland and Scotland, education was mainly teacher led. Systems were less centrally dominated, with teachers having a fair amount of control over pedagogy and assessment. In these countries, tensions were about the anticipation of new reforms following a global standards agenda. Specific projects showed that their pedagogies owed much to child-centred European literature on learning from the past, such as that of Pestalozzi and Freinet.

The CLASP Project: documenting the 'what' of creative learning

We were able to provide some abstract concepts such as relevance, control, ownership and innovation that were exemplified by extensive research data from our past projects about creative teaching (Woods, 1990; Woods, 1993; Woods, 1995; Woods and Jeffrey, 1996; Jeffrey and Woods, 2003). These concepts are also characteristic of creative learning, relevance, control and ownership of learning processes, and innovation. We concluded that if the teaching is relevant to children's lives, worlds, cultures and interests, they are more likely to be able to control their own learning processes. While relevance aids identification, motivation, excitement and enthusiasm, control leads to ownership of the knowledge that results. If relevance, control and ownership apply, there is an increased chance of creative learning, and when something new is created, there is significant change or transformation in the pupil, ie: an innovative experience (Woods, 2002).

The broad objectives of the Creative Learning and Student Perspectives (CLASP) were:

- to identify teachers' and students' strategies for developing creative learning in educational contexts

■ to examine the effectiveness of incorporating student perspectives into the teaching and learning process

■ to highlight the advantages to be gained for the quality of teaching and learning by examining cross-European creative pedagogic practices

The innovative nature of the project lay in combining two cross-national policy developments, an interest in the expansion of creativity and the effectiveness gained from incorporating student perspectives into pedagogic practices. The process was reciprocal in that the development of creative learning enhanced creative practices and encouraged student commitment.

CLASP's main activity involved nine months of qualitative research incorporating fieldwork observations, conversations, interviews with teachers and pupils, and development work concerned with creative learning in the educational sites. This was interspersed with regular electronic communication and meetings with partners to compare, research, record and evaluate critical analyses, research data and processes. The researchers acted as participant observers to interpret contexts and situations. They also engaged in dialogues with teachers and pupils about their research analysis. The main features of creative learning, across the partners, were real programmes and critical events. The main effect of creative learning was upon relationships.

Real programmes and critical events

In the main, schools and teachers were the instigators of specific school and class creativity programmes. They determined the processes by which children experienced creative learning. They also constructed the quality of the creative learning environments in which the pupils worked, together with the influence of resources and community partners.

One of the major strategies across most of the partners' reports was the instigation of 'real' programmes, which were similar to 'critical events'. These were designed to affect the interest and commitment of pupils, as well as to influence institutional and local area policy. They conformed to the structure of a critical event, which goes through well-defined stages of conceptualisation, preparation and planning, divergence, convergence, consolidation and celebration (Woods, 1993).

According to the children, these real programmes had a social and educational reality that legitimised their involvement as social beings. The decision by schools to create a critical event established a special time period, or project within the school timetable, which in some cases was integrated within the rest of the curriculum programme. In other cases, the critical events were treated separately, although they often involved the use of other curriculum subjects or directly influenced separate subject study. They also involved a considerable amount of external engagement from advisors, artists, specialist funders, workshop providers, project specialists and visitors.

The events included school environment improvements and analysis as in Milton Keynes and Cadiz; computer toy constructions for major competitions in Dublin; re-enactments of social issues in Cadiz; and the examination of lives from different cultures in Glasgow. They either replaced the designated curriculum or were incorporated into an existing programmes to enhance them: there were designated specialist weeks to a particular curriculum subject right across the school (Milton Keynes) or the allocation of a specific week to a creative project (Cadiz, Glasgow). The events often involved strategic co-operations with external partners and organisations in the community, such as dancers, artists, sculptors, actors and environmental workers (Milton Keynes and Innsbruck).

With the community's help, the Innsbruck school (Raggl, 2006) prepared the outside environment as a physical adventure for learners in which curriculum programmes were enacted and learning took place. At a Dublin school, one of the classes was transformed into a Victorian classroom, in which the children used slates and worked in silence for the day (Sugrue, 2006). In one of the Cadiz Early Years schools (Vallinjas-Porras, 2006), the pupils regularly held cultural events such as weddings, divorces and celebratory meals, initiations such as baptisms and confirmations and other cultural equivalents. The Glasgow (Smyth, 2006) pupils raised funds for an outing to a well-known beauty spot by making and selling cakes and having fairs, as well as booking their own coaches and tours and organising lunches. They marketed both the outings and the learning activities for the day. One of the Milton Keynes schools had a Maths and Design and Technology week (Jeffrey and Craft, 2006). Events included visits to local zoos, football clubs, pizza parlours and other schools, and specialists were employed to run large workshops in the school hall or grounds or in the kitchens. Another Milton Keynes school planned a Sounds in the Environment programme: one class worked with the National Theatre for two terms, another with a specialist dance teacher and the whole school was engaged in improving the school environment with the help of artists, sculptors and community workers.

The outcomes of these events were similar to those in Peter Woods' (1993) critical events. He found that

> outcomes for learners included positive attitudes to learning, new found confidences, motivation for learning, enhanced disposition, and skills in listening to others and being listened to, self discovery, realisation of abilities and interests, a 'coming out' of a new found self, blending in to previous impenetrable cultures and emotional development. (*ibid*, p. 141)

Influences on relationships

A notable outcome of these creative teaching and learning strategies was the change in relationships and innovative developments in interactive engagements. The Glasgow project emphasised the importance of relevant teacher strategies for the bilingual children they taught. These pupils brought the environment and local culture into the classroom as well as exploring it *in situ*. In Dublin, the emotional work done by the teachers resulted in higher levels of trust and an exchange of skills took place between teachers and children.

Young children in Cadiz were encouraged to play a full part in daily democratic decision-making and to take responsibility for those decisions at the expense of themselves and in support of others and collective decision-making. They developed relationships by solving their own disputes and closer home and school relationships made a holistic environment for learning. A major feature of the Innsbruck research site was involving parents as partners, peer assistance and collaborations between parents, teachers and students acting as co-creators. Social development was achieved by ownership of the space, relationship responsibility and social obligations to classroom democratic practices, role-play and empathy (Cadiz and Innsbruck), and the promotion of participatory practices (Milton Keynes, Cadiz, Innsbruck, Glasgow).

Conclusion

Although the European projects involved in this research were based in different cultures, they drew upon a common European literature in which learning is relevant, the children have some ownership and control, and innovation is often attached to their experience. The influence of this literature was more prevalent in the Austrian, English and Spanish contexts, but there were individual teachers in the Irish and Scottish projects who injected its influence into their pedagogy.

The pace of reform differs from country to country. English policy is in the vanguard of raising achievement through extensive testing and target setting and there is now government support for creativity policies in England. Ireland and Scotland are following this path by building on their past similar practices, although Scotland is concerned about maintaining a balance between performance-based policies and creative learning. Both Spain and Austria, however, are responding to the global standards agenda. This agenda is introducing national testing in 2007 and downgrading teacher assessment, which may reduce a more general practice of creative teaching and learning. The situation is fluid, with some teachers and schools finding it easier than others to appropriate the reforms while maintaining creative pedagogic values (Jeffrey and Woods, 2003). Ireland has the least supportive context for creative teaching and learning since these practices have had relatively little influence in the past.

Although ethnographic, small-scale studies, such the CLASP project, do not have a broad enough sample to show general cultural pedagogic preferences and therefore cultural differences, they may contribute to the development of creative teaching and learning. First, they can provide examples for countries hosting creative projects, with these countries appropriating individual teachers and schools who may be able to influence their own creativity discourse. Secondly, by indicating a global interest in creative teaching and learning, individual cultures can be stimulated to show an interest in and influence a global discourse on the subject, even if this is less powerful than being able to set a global standards agenda.

In methodological terms, the CLASP study focused on 'individuals and groups of learners situated within a larger cultural context' (Osborn, 2004, p 269). There was a loosely coupled framework within which each partner used an ethnographic fieldwork methodology and a grounded theory approach to analyse and report on their own projects. The co-ordinators of the project then carried out an analytical synthesis of their reports to construct the final cross-cultural research report (Troman and Jeffrey, 2007).

We aimed to take part in cross-cultural, collaborative research within the new tradition. The goal of the new tradition is to 'contribute to a collective understanding of the inter-relatedness of the various cultural factors concerned and the danger of crude policy borrowing' (Osborn, 2004, p. 268). Our ethnographic study attempted to unravel the complex interplay of factors, personal, social and structural, that influence children engagement with learning. Further approaches along the lines of the methodology of the CLASP project provide a way for these aims to be realised. At the same time, they show how meaningful and relevant cross-cultural conceptualisations can be painstakingly constructed.

References

Alexander, R (2001) Border Crossings. *Comparative Education*, 37 (4) p507-523

Broadfoot, P (2000) Comparative Education for the 21st century: retrospect and prospect. *Comparative Education*, 36(3) p357-371

Broadfoot, P (2002a) Editorial: structure and agency in education: the role of comparative education. *Comparative Education*, 38(1) p5-6

Broadfoot, P (2002b) Editorial: educational policy in comparative perspective. *Comparative Education*, 38(2), 133-135

Jeffrey, B (2005) ESRC Report of the UK Creative Learning and Student Perspectives (CLASP) Project ESRC http://www.esrcsocietytoday.ac.uk/ (March 2005)

Jeffrey, B (2006) (ed) *Creative learning practices: European experiences*, London: Tufnell

Jeffrey, B and Craft, A (2006) Creative learning and possibility thinking, in B Jeffrey (ed), *Creative learning practices: European Experiences*. London: Tufnell Press, p49-64

Jeffrey, B and Woods, P (2003) *The Creative School: A framework for success, quality and effectiveness*. London: Routledge/Falmer

Osborn, M (2004) New methodologies for comparative research? Establishing 'constants' and 'contexts' in educational experience. *Oxford Review of Education*, 30(2) p265-285

Raggl, A (2006)The Bridge School – Creative learning as community learning, in B Jeffrey (ed) *Creative learning practices: European Experiences*. London: Tufnell Press, p34-46

Smyth, G (2006) Bi-lingual learner's perspectives on school and society in Scotland. In B Jeffrey (ed), *Creative learning practices: European Experiences*. London: Tufnell Press p63-86

Sugrue, C (2006) Structure and agency in the construction of creative teaching and learning: a view from the margins. In B Jeffrey (ed), *Creative learning practices: European Experiences*. London: Tufnell Press, p87-108

Troman, G and Jeffrey, B (2005) Providing a framework for a 'shared repertoire' in a cross-national research project. In GTroman, B. Jeffrey, G Walford (eds) *Researching Education Policy: Ethnographic experiences: A Methodological Reader* Vol 11 London: Tufnell Press/Oxford:Elsevier, pp 207-226

Troman, G and Jeffrey, B (2007) Qualitative data analysis in cross-cultural projects. *Comparative Education* 43 (4)

Vallinjas-Porras, R (2006) Creative learning in an infant school in B Jeffrey (ed) *Creative learning practices: European Experiences*. London: Tufnell Press, p13-33

Woods, P (1990) *Teacher Skills and Strategies*. London: Falmer

Woods, P (1993) *Critical events in teaching and learning*. London: Falmer

Woods, P (1995) *Creative Teachers in Primary Schools*. Buckingham: Open University Press

Woods, P (2002), Teaching and Learning in the New Millenium. In C. Sugrue (ed) *Developing Teaching and Teachers: International Research Perspectives*. London: Falmer, p73-91

Woods, P and Jeffrey, B (1996) *Teachable Moments: The Art Of Creative Teaching In Primary Schools*. Buckingham: Open University Press

6

Teachers' perceptions of creative learning in India

Mahender Reddy Sarsani

Education and creativity

As the world's political, economic, scientific and technological, social and cultural spheres have changed, educating the young appropriately has become a priority in every society. There is a growing sense that the challenges and jobs of tomorrow will require an education of better quality than that which most students receive today (UNESCO, 1998). Craft and Dugal (1997) argue that

> the end of the twentieth century is witnessing a massive shift in attitudes to and the importance of, creativity and imagination in our everyday lives and domains of knowledge. We need transformation, at both a personal and a system level.

In the UK, the NACCCE (1999) report highlights the importance of creativity, not only for education but as an essential vehicle for economic, social and individual development. Jeffrey and Craft (2001) describe the context of the current drive to foster and value creativity as universal, where creativity is seen as relevant and necessary in a wide variety of social, economic, cultural and political contexts. Craft (2000) points out that 'the changes in information and communication technology bring enormous possibilities to schools as institutions, and open many doors to how children may be supported in learning in the future'. The current competitive discourse has meant that many institutions and organisations are encouraging creativity in order to improve their performance and to find ways in which to diversify in order to expand (Craft, 2005).

43

Creative people will be a valuable resource in the rapid process of change, especially of technological change, which has gripped the world in recent years (McLeod and Cropley, 1989). Creativity in children needs to be encouraged so that they become successful members of society (Chaube and Chaube, 1994), and the educational environment should value the creative thinking potential of its school children. Giving due recognition to the phenomenon and importance of creativity will enable individuals to develop their abilities to the maximum, and may help to prevent stagnation and inertia in society (Shan, 2005).

Creativity – its recognition and development in India

The issue of developing creativity in school children is challenging to teachers, schools and educational administrators, as well as to researchers in the fields of education and psychology. In many countries teachers have been criticised and schools blamed for not providing an environment in which creativity can be nurtured. The focus of the education system is on examination results rather than on the actual process of learning (Raina, 1989; Chadha, 1990; Rather, 1998).

The education system and its unrealistic syllabi are so taxing that for much of the time creative imaginations are suppressed and blocked. School programmes in India do not give due recognition to the kinds of educational experiences and proper environments that are essential for the development of creative potential (Rather, 1998). Instead, teachers tend to encourage pupils they regard as intelligent and who give them the correct answers to their questions whereas little encouragement is given to children who are creative (Khire, 1977).

Educational researchers, commissions and committees in India have criticised educational practices for failing to foster creativity among students and ignoring the development of the imagination and independent thinking. Although they have made numerous recommendations to reduce the academic burden on students, no changes have been implemented.

The development of Indian creativity tests and review studies

Since 1950, there has been serious research in the field of creativity, although for a long time it was mostly in the realm of psychology. Passi *et al* (1982) report that in 1956, Bhattacharya conducted the first Indian study in the area of correlates of creativity (*ibid*, p.11), an area which later attracted the attention of many more Indian researchers. During the 1970s, a number of tests for creativity were developed (Passi, 1973; Mehdi, 1973; Majumdar, 1973;

Kundley, 1977), although many of these were formulated for measuring creativity in schoolchildren in English and Hindi. More recently educators have started doing systematic research on creativity hoping to add to national development through the efficient use of multi-faceted talent (Rather, 1998).

Research on creativity in India has focused on the construction of tests of creativity and correlational studies of creativity with self-concept, school climate, intelligence, personality, achievement and motivation. Several comparative studies of government and private schools have reported that the performance of private school students as higher than that of government school students in terms of creative thinking ability.

Creative thinking – Indian teachers' views and definitions

Arts education remains one on the most neglected areas of the school curriculum in India (Singh, 1991): furthermore, teachers have reported that creativity is hardly included in the arts. During teacher training, teacher educators' awareness of the need for creativity in the classroom is limited to the need for innovation and divergent, creative thinking while learning subject-matter content (Raina and Raina, 1981).

Studies of teachers' views and attitudes about the promotion of creativity are important as evidence to assist in promoting change. Yet, with a few notable exceptions (eg Raina and Raina, 1971; Raina and Raina, 1981; Singh and Das, 1989; Sarsani, 1999), there have been no in-depth studies considering the effects of schooling on creativity, or teachers' perceptions of creativity or how to promote creativity at primary level. Studies of teachers' views of creativity are as rare as research reports on creativity from abroad (eg. Torrance, 1965; Ohuche, 1986; Popescu-Nevianu and Cretsu, 1986; Fryer, 1989).

The author's research (Sarsani,1999) focused on teachers' views of creativity and their classroom practices in India. My findings showed that teachers valued creativity and had established criteria for the definition of creativity and for identifying creative children. The majority of teachers reported that creative thinking was included in their teacher training, mainly under the auspices of educational psychology. The overall knowledge and understanding of the teachers about creativity was good. They also had positive attitudes, although their knowledge of creative techniques in the classroom, such as brainstorming and Synectics, was limited.

The Indian teachers in the study had similar conceptions of creative thinking to those identified among British teachers by Fryer (1989). Both groups saw creativity as inspiration, imagination, having original ideas and self-expression. The Indian teachers viewed creative thinking as a process involving divergent thinking and innovation, ranking unconscious aspects of the processes lowest. As with British teachers, the Indian teachers' views are closer to the humanistic than the psychoanalytic approach.

Creative thinking – teachers' attitudes towards the creative child

Torrance (1965) used his Ideal Pupil checklist to explore the attitudes of over a thousand teachers from the United States, Germany, India, Greece and the Philippines towards the creative child (see Table 1). He concluded that teachers in all five cultures under-valued the creative child. Undue reward was given to courtesy, doing work on time, obedience, popularity and willingness to accept the judgement of authorities.

This study has been replicated by Raina and Raina (1971) in India, and Ohuche (1986) in Nigeria. Their results show that teachers attach a great deal of importance to industriousness, sincerity, obedience and meeting deadlines. The attitudes of the Indian teachers matched those reflected in Torrance's 1965 study.

Ohuche (1986) argues that since the Nigerian educational system is highly competitive and examination results oriented, teachers strive to prepare students to excel in examinations. As is the custom in their culture, conformity, obedience and consideration for others are required. Similarly, Raina and Raina (1971) argue that the system of education in India is authoritarian and traditional. Indian society is conservative and authoritarian, and obedience and sincerity are demanded. The creative person must be open to new ideas, but must examine everything before accepting it as their own. Intellectual honesty, sincerity and independence are not compatible with a conformist society dominated by external examinations: they tend to bring the individual into conflict and to isolate the creative child (Raina and Raina, 1971).

A study in the UK by Fryer (1989) was designed to provide a comprehensive map of teachers' views on creativity, together with a more detailed investigation of the views of a representative sub-sample. Following unstructured exploratory interviews and pilot work, a questionnaire was devised for respondents to complete. Teachers were asked to identify the five characteristics that they valued most and the five that they valued least. At the top of the list of the most highly rated characteristics were: consideration for others, being socially well adjusted, self-confidence, independence in thinking and curiosity (see Table 6.1).

Studied by		Torrance (1965)					Raina & Raina (1971)	Ohuche (1986)	Fryer (1989)
Sample drawn form		Teachers					Teacher Educators	Secondary School teachers	School & college teachers
Sample Size (N)		264 94 375 94 147					100	127	1028
S.No	Characteristics	US	Germany	India	Greece	Philippines	India	Nigeria	UK
1	Adventurous	-	10	-	-	-	-	-	-
2	Affectionate	-	-	9	-	10	-	8	-
3	Altruistic	-	-	-	8	-	-	-	-
4	Attempts difficult tasks	-	5	-	-	-	-	-	-
5	Considerate of others	4	-	-	-	5	2	4	1
6	Courteous	-	-	4	10	3	5	7	-
7	Curious	2	7	1	-	-	9	-	5
8	Determination	7	-	10	-	-	-	-	-
9	Does work on time	-	-	3	-	6	6	-	-
10	Energetic	-	-	-	1	-	-	-	-
11	Healthy	-	9	5	7	4	-	6	-
12	Independent in judgement	-	6	-	-	-	-	-	-
13	Independent thinking	1	4	-	-	-	10	-	4
14	Industrious	5	3	8	-	1	1	1	-
15	Non-conforming	-	-	-	5	-	-	-	-
16	Obedient	-	-	2	-	2	4	3	-
17	Receptive to other's ideas	6	-	-	-	-	3	-	-
18	Remember well	-	-	-	6	8	-	-	-
19	Self-confident	-	-	6	9	7	-	5	3
20	Self-starter	8	8	7	-	-	-	-	-
21	Sense of humour	3	2	-	-	-	-	-	-
22	Sincere	9	1	-	4	-	8	2	-
23	Socially well adjusted	-	-	-	-	-	-	-	2
24	Strive for distant goals	-	-	-	2	-	-	-	-
25	Thorough	10	-	-	3	-	-	-	-
26	Well liked by peers	-	-	-	-	-	7	-	-
27	Willing to accept judgements of authorities	-	-	-	-	9	-	-	-

Table 6.1: The most favoured characteristics by various cultural groups in different studies

Studied by		Torrance (1965)					Raina & Raina (1971)	Ohuche (1986)	Fryer (1989)
Sample drawn form		Teachers					Teacher Educators	Secondary School teachers	School & college teachers
Sample Size (N)		264 94 375 94 147					100	127	1028
S.No	Characteristics	US	Germany	India	Greece	Philippines	India	Nigeria	UK
1	A good guesser	-	-	-	-	-	6	-	-
2	Always asks questions	-	-	-	-	-	9	-	-
3	Bashful	-	-	-	-	3	8	2	-
4	Critical of others	-	-	-	-	-	4	-	-
5	Disturbs classes	4	1	1	5	2	10	9	4
6	Domineering	2	5	-	4	-	-	3	5
7	Faultfinding	5	2	2	-	5	5	4	-
8	Haughty and self-satisfied	1	4	-	1	-	-	-	2
9	Like to work alone	-	-	-	-	-	1	-	-
10	Negativistic	3	-	-	2	-	-	5	1
11	Non-conformist	-	-	-	-	-	3	1	-
12	Regressive	-	-	4	-	-	2	-	-
13	Stubborn and obstinate	-	-	5	-	1	-	7	3
14	Talkative	-	3	3	-	2	-	8	-
15	Timed	-	-	-	3	4	7	6	-

Table 6.2: The least favoured characteristics by various cultural groups in different studies

Despite the above results, the British teachers in this study seemed more willing to encourage creativity than those involved in earlier studies (Fryer, 1989). Fryer quotes some examples from her study of what the teachers said, 'I try to be a creative teacher; I would like to be one; my goal for the children is self-sufficiency'.

All the cultures agreed that the characteristics which teachers should discourage included: disturbing classes, domineering (except India and Philippines) and fault finding (except Greece and UK). The characteristics exclusive to Indian teachers were: being critical of others, liking to work alone, regressing, being a good guesser and always asking questions (see Table 6.2).

Since teachers consistently evoke attitudes and reactions in students which are similar to their own (Tausch, 1960), children will benefit if their teachers' attitudes are favourable (Mirman, 1964). As Torrance (1965) demonstrated, it is generally believed that when teachers have a positive attitude to creativity this fosters creativity in pupils. Singh (1985) found that unfavourable or negative attitudes by teachers towards creative learning depress the children's creative thinking (Singh and Das, 1989).

Singh and Das (1989) attempted to assess the attitude of teachers in India. In their study, all the teachers have favourable attitudes towards creative learning but unfavourable attitudes towards creative teaching, except in the case of post-higher secondary teachers. They conclude that, although teachers wish their pupils to learn creativity, they do not like to teach pupils in a creative manner. Either they do not know creative methods of teaching or do not have the will to teach creatively. In the case of post-higher secondary teachers, their more favourable attitudes may be due to a recognition of the value of creativity in education.

Creative thinking – teachers' views on development and obstacles

In India, the notion of creative learning is less familiar to educational psychologists than creative thinking. Sarsani's 1999 study revealed that creative thinking can be developed through adopting various teaching methods. These include:

- providing students with new problems to generate new and unfamiliar solution

- improvising apparatus

- asking divergent questions in teaching

- giving more scope to students to ask questions (through training in activities or organising programmes)

- using visual aids

- having discussions

- telling life-histories of great people.

As to factors assisting in the development of creativity, both the Indian teachers studied by Sarsani (1999) and the British teachers studied by Fryer (1989), put building self-confidence in first place. Having a creative teacher was ranked in second and third places respectively. Indian teachers perceived good pupil relations, encouraging experimentation and developing curiosity as important factors. They did not believe that informal teaching assists in developing creativity. In a formal traditional teaching system, such as in India, the teachers are restricted to working within the boundaries or framework of the curriculum – so that it is understandable that they are used to teaching formally rather informally.

Sarsani's study (1999) also showed that Indian teachers often fail to develop creativity among their students, despite their enthusiasm to do so, because of obstacles with teachers, students and schools.

- At teacher level, the major obstacles were the overloaded syllabus: the stress on completion of the syllabus: an over-emphasis on preparing the pupils for examinations; a heavy teaching load; lack of time; lack of recognition and appreciation of teachers' work; emphasis on the lecture method; and inadequate training in creativity and its development.

- The teachers believed that the obstacles at pupil level were: the children's lack of experience and their participation in the classroom as passive, silent spectators; a tendency to rote learn; a lack of motivation; general poor performance; unequal aptitudes; poor family background; no parental care or encouragement; and parental illiteracy.

- The teachers reported obstacles at school level, such as inadequate resources; instructional materials; conflicts over curricular demands; unsuitable accommodation and inadequate funds. In the interviews, the obstacles identified were shortage of time for teachers, an overloaded syllabus, short lesson periods, lack of laboratory facilities, government policies, lack of knowledge among the administrators, pressure on teachers to complete the syllabus, and other distractions from teaching, such as enumeration and frequent election duties.

The results are similar to those found among British teachers (Fryer, 1989). Inadequate resources and preparation time, large classes, excessive non-teaching workloads, an excessive teaching load and unsuitable accommodation were all major obstacles reported in British educational institutions.

Conclusion

Indian society is conservative and authoritarian, and the system of education is authoritarian and traditional. Creativity is viewed by teachers as inspirational or imaginative, based on cognition. While its importance is valued for individual development and society in the future, teachers are hindered by obstacles such as a lack of resources and materials, the curriculum and examination system, inappropriate accommodation, large class sizes, and a general lack of freedom in teaching and of support for developing creativity. Pupils tend to be unmotivated, passive, and lacking in experience and confidence. They perform poorly and learn by rote. Teachers also require more training, particularly to develop practical creative ideas (Sarsani, 1999, 2006).

Teachers who are keen to develop creativity prefer to teach in a variety of ways and to value every child's contribution (Fryer, 1996; Sarsani, 2006). It is evident from the literature that teachers can promote creativity if they are willing to do it. What is required is:

- a positive, open, receptive and accepting attitude
- a congenial environment
- a warm and friendly atmosphere
- value given to students' responses
- the encouragement of self-initiated learning

The research studies discussed in this chapter reveal that there is a need to organise special training programmes, conferences, seminars and symposia, orientation and refresher courses, workshops, books and journals for teachers in India. These would enable Indian teachers to keep abreast of the knowledge and understanding necessary for the development of creativity in students.

References

Chadha, N K (1990) Creativity, Intelligence and scholastic Achievement: A Residual study. *Indian Educational Review,* XXV(3), 84-85

Chaube, S P and Chaube, A (1994) *Educational psychology.* Agra (India): Lakshmi Narain Agarwal educational publishers

Craft, A (2000) *Creativity Across the Primary Curriculum.* London: Routledge – Falmer

Craft, A (2005) *Creativity in schools: Tensions and Dilemmas.* London: Routledge

Craft, A and Dugal, J (1997) Challenges to vision and creativity, in A Craft, J Dugal, G Dyer, B Jeffrey and T Lyons (eds), *Can you teach creativity?* Nottingham (England): Education Now

Fryer, M (1989) Teachers' views on creativity. Unpublished PhD thesis, Leeds: Leeds Metropolitan University

Fryer, M (1996) *Creative Teaching and Learning.* London: Paul Chapman Publishing Ltd

Jeffrey, B and Craft, A (2001) The universalization of creativity in education. In A Craft, B Jeffrey and M Leibling (eds), *Creativity in education.* London: Continuum, p1-13

Khire, U (1977) Education for Creativity. *Journal of Indian Education* 3 p26-30

Kundley, M B (1977) A Test of Literary Creativity in Marathi. Doctoral Thesis Nagpur: Nagpur University

Majumdar, S K (1973) *Scientific Creativity*. New Delhi: NCERT (Mimeographed)

McLeod, J and Cropley, A (1989), *Fostering Academic Excellence*. Oxford: Pergamon Press

Mehdi, B (1973, 1985a) *Manual of Verbal Test of Creative Thinking* (2nd ed). Aligarh: Publisher Mrs. Q. Fatima

Mirman, N (1964) Teacher Qualifications for Educating the Gifted. *Gifted Child Quarterly*, 8 (123-128)

National Advisory Committee on Creative and Cultural Education (NACCCE) (1999) *All our Futures: creativity, culture and education*. London: DFEE

Ohuche, N M (1986) The ideal pupil as perceived by Nigerian (Igbo) teachers and Torrance's creative personality. *International Review of Education* 32 p192-94

Passi, B K (1973, 1979) *Passi tests of creativity (Verbal and Non-verbal)*. Agra (India): National Psychological Corporation

Passi, B. K., Sansanwal, D. N. and Jarial, G. S. (1982). *Creativity in Education: Its correlates* (1st Edition). Agra (India): National Psychological Corporation

Popescu-Nevianu, P and Cretsu, T (1986) cited in M Fryer and J A Collings (1991) Study of teachers' creative abilities. *Revue Roumaine Des Sciences Sociales*, 30(2), 129-34 (selective English translation by Ludmilla Lewis)

Raina, M K (1989) *Social Change and Changes in Creative Functioning*. New Delhi: National Council of Educational Research and Training

Raina, M K and Raina, V K (1981) Teacher-educator competency in creativity. *Indian Educational Review,* XVI (3) p103-109

Raina, T N and Raina, M K (1971) Perception of Teacher educators in India about the Ideal Pupil. *The Journal of Educational Research*, 64(7) p303-308

Rather, A R (1998) *Creativity: Its Recognition and Development*. New Delhi: Sarup and Sons

Sarsani, M R (1999) Exploring the promotion of creative thinking among secondary school students in India. Unpublished PhD thesis London: University of London

Sarsani, M R (2006) *Creativity in Schools*. New Delhi: Sarup and Sons

Shan, H R (2005) *Identification and development of creativity.* New Delhi: Commonwealth Publishers

Singh, B S (1991) *Secondary school Curriculum In India*. Delhi: Penman Publishers

Singh, R P (1985) Attitudes of high school teachers towards creative learning and teaching. *Prachi – Journal of Psycho-Cultural Dimensions*, 1 p7-12

Singh, R P and Das, M (1989) Attitude of teachers towards creative learning and Teaching. *Indian Educational Review,* XXIV(2) p120-124

Tausch, A (1960) Empirische Untersuchungen Uber Die Wirkung Verschiedner Eriehungshalt Ungen im Erlebnis Von Kinder. *Z. Exp. Ang. Psychol.*, 7 p472-491

Torrance, E P (1965) *Rewarding creative behaviour experiments in classroom creativity*. NJ: Prentice-Hall

UNESCO. (1998) *World education report: Teachers and teaching in a changing world*. Paris: UNESCO Publishing

7

Mixed-methods research in documenting creative learning

David S Martin

Introduction

Compared with numerous other topics in education, research on creativity, creative learning and teaching for creativity is still in its infancy. One reason is that the concept of creativity, lacking firm definition, has been elusive. Another is that several countries' public policies since the 1990s have resulted in a revived interest in convergent thinking, with fact-based education ruling the day. Some practitioner-researchers have been discouraged by this return to a positivist paradigm, since quantitative approaches have not yielded credible results, particularly in relation to outcomes such as creative learning which are hard to measure. Qualitative methods, on the other hand, have been saddled with a negative reputation in the study of creativity due to the accusation that such methods lack objectivity, are subjective and 'soft'.

This chapter calls for the reaffirming of a combined, or mixed-methods, methodology for practitioner-researchers studying creative learning, in particular with children aged 3-11. The powerful combination of both qualitative and quantitative methodologies comprises a combined paths or mixed methods research approach for documenting what is truly happening within the dynamics of living classrooms (Creswell, 2003).

Ascribing meaning

An essential principle for practitioner-researchers to understand is that human beings always identify the 'real' world of experience imperfectly, and can only approximate that reality when they carry out investigations. Hammersley (1992) speaks of using a 'concept of subtle reality', which is the closest approximation that can be achieved as evidence is collected. Another principle is that creative products may be viewed as the result of the creator's attempt to make meaning.

Jeffrey (2005) points out that the key characteristics in the conception of creative learning are similar to those applied to creative teaching – namely relevance, control, ownership and innovation. He expands on ownership as the pupil learning for herself, rather than for the teacher, and explains that control is applied to self-motivation as opposed to extrinsic factors. The practitioner-researcher who is documenting creative learning must investigate both how the learner makes meaning in these ways, and how the teacher sets the stage for that kind of learning to occur. Specifically, Jeffrey (*ibid*) indicates that research foci should be on connection-making; possibility thinking and knowledge; playing with ideas; discussion and evaluation of options; risk-taking; the valuing of uncertainty; and the construction of alternative solutions to problems. The practitioner-researcher needs to investigate the varied roles played by all individuals engaged in the process of creative learning.

Criteria for selection of methods

The practitioner-researcher needs to apply certain criteria in order to have a systematic approach to the selection of research methods. This chapter suggests six criteria, taking the form of six questions, for choosing methodologies. The criteria are intended to be descriptive rather than to connote any positive or negative value.

The practitioner-researcher should ask whether potential research methods are:

- *Obtrusive or unobtrusive?* An obtrusive method either clearly occupies classroom time, directly influences the classroom context or is one of which the research subjects (pupils or teachers) are aware. The term 'unobtrusive' refers to data collection of which pupils are unaware and involves more naturalistic observational methods (Greene and Hogan, 2005).

- *Norm-referenced or criterion-referenced?* Some methods are standardised on a norm group, leading to results which compare research subjects against the performance of that norm group. Others are based only on the performance of individual research subjects in relation to some set of criteria, and thus no focus is placed on comparing pupils with other pupils or on comparing teachers with other teachers.

■ *Cognitive or affective or psychomotor?* Some methods focus on thought and knowledge, some on emotions and attitudes and some on an aspect of physical performance. A balance of research methods along the cognitive, psychomotor and affective dimensions of creative learning would provide a fuller picture than a focus on only one aspect.

■ *Group-administered or individually-administered?* Some methods are designed to be carried out with groups of research subjects at the same time, while others are intended to be given to individuals alone. A combination of both dimensions allows for an examination of individual performances separate from interaction within a group.

■ *Objective or subjective?* Some educational researchers regard quantifiable and/or machine-scorable data as the only truly objective methods, regarding other methods as subjective and therefore inferior or not credible. This dichotomy, described by Crotty (2005) as 'the great divide', is, however, essentially false. The definition of objective in this sense may be applied to any research method whose outcome or result will not vary according to who administers it – no personal bias can come into play. Objectivism and subjectivism are epistemological views concerned with providing a philosophical grounding for deciding what kinds of knowledge are possible. Objectivism sees things exist as 'meaningful entities independently of consciousness and experience' (*ibid*, p5). In subjectivism, the way of seeing things is in the making of meaning, which is a subjective act. What is important is that embedded in these stances are assumptions underpinning how we think about our research, do our researching and how we present our research outcomes (Burnard, 2006).

■ *Formative or summative?* While these two terms are more frequently used in relation to pupil evaluation or assessment more than in research, they have their place in research. A formative technique is one where the results will be used by someone – frequently a teacher – to change instruction in some way. A summative technique is one where the primary interest is in reporting the result. If research is regarded as a chain of events in which the links are interrelated, one researcher's results for a particular moment may be summative, but can become formative if it is later used by educators to change instruction or by other researchers for their own follow-up studies.

A balanced application of criteria in the selection of methods for conducting research into creative learning is recommended. This would benefit the pupils as well as the teachers who teach them.

Variety in research methods

A research plan which incorporates a variety of measures, drawn from both quantitative and qualitative domains, should assure the researcher of a fruitful, multiple-pathway approach. Eleven possible methodological options for studies of creative learning are:

1. *Observation scales for teacher and for pupil behaviours.* In this method, the researcher first specifies which particular behaviours are of interest. For pupils, a checklist of creative behavioural characteristics during classroom discussions, for example, could be used both before and after some experimental intervention. Separately, in investigating teacher behaviours, standardised instruments such as the Classroom Observation Checklist for teacher-fostering of creative and critical thinking may be used (Winocur, 1991). Trained observers systematically record the behaviours of pupils or teachers according to pre-set criteria, usually in the form of a list of behaviours, followed by a scale such as one to five, with a numerical value being attached to each point on that continuum. This method is particularly appropriate for pupils aged 3-11. To apply the six selection criteria from the previous section, this methodology is: unobtrusive; may be cognitive, affective or psychomotor, depending on the types of targeted behaviours; criterion-referenced; individually-administered; and it can be fairly objective if the observers are well trained to an acceptable level of inter-rater reliability.

2. *Problem-solving scenario.* Another effective way to gain insight into pupils' ability to think creatively is to present them with a hypothetical situation and ask them to compose a solution (orally for ages 3-7 or on paper for ages 8-11). This method is most effective when done prior to, and then after, any educational intervention; it gives insight into pupils' thought processes because they are constructing their responses to a given scenario.

For research purposes, the results may be subjected to content-analyses and frequency counts for recurrent themes. A hypothetical problem could be posed to pupils, such as:

> You and a friend are going on a long car journey with your family; you know that you need to find a way not to be bored. What activity idea could you invent, using whatever things are available in the car, so that you will not become bored?

A content analysis will then reveal trends in these data for discussion (Martin, Craft, and Zhang, 2001).

3. *Interactive oral interview.* The structured interactive oral interview is a valid means for assessing quickly, yet incisively, what a pupil does and does not understand about a particular topic. It is also useful for assessing her/his response to a given situation or stimulus. In creative learning research, the interviewer emphasises why and how questions to lead the interviewee to elaborate and may then pose probing questions, such as, 'Why do you say that?', or 'Please explain what you mean'. This elicits valuable additional data from children between the ages of 3 and 11.

4. *Focus Group.* As a follow-up to individual interviews, or as a group assessment of interactive understanding, a focus group can provide insights that are not obtainable in other ways. An effective group provides some advance information on the topic which will be the focus of discussion. The researcher assembles the group, poses the first question and encourages members of the group to participate, building interactively on one another's responses with follow-up commentary, before moving the group on to the next question. It is essential for the process to be recorded so that content analyses of the focus group interaction can subsequently be carried out. Variations on interactive focus groups may include web-based discussion groups that are asynchronous, synchronous live computer-based chatrooms, video conferencing or other webcam-based forums. These eliminate the problem of geographic distance between research subjects.

5. *Standardised examinations of academic achievement.* The practitioner-researcher might not consider a standardised examination of academic achievement in literacy or mathematics to be a measure of creative learning. However, if one of the outcomes of a research

project is to bring about creative learning approaches in the class-room, its effects on academic achievement would definitely be of interest.

6. *Standardised assessments of cognitive or affective components of creativity.* There are standardised instruments for assessment of creativity, such as the Torrance tests. One international comparative study made use of the Raven's *Standard Progressive Matrices* (1959) as a recognised assessment of reasoning skills. Statistically significant differences were found in favour of the experimental groups from both countries participating in the study (Martin, Craft and Zhang, 2001).

7. *Analysis of pupil artefacts.* The analysis of items produced by pupils – such as art work, essays, physical models, oral presentations and portfolios – provides another means of collecting valuable data on pupil creativity. Artefacts produced by pupils either individually or in groups may be analysed according to a set of pre-determined criteria. These could include the artefact's innovativeness, clarity, collabora-tion in the case of a group project, thoroughness, expression and detail. The most complete analysis of student products occurs when several judges are used; the form of analysis may be through an analytic rubric, applied by judges who have previously reached some predetermined acceptable level of inter-rater reliability.

8. *Case study.* The case study of particular individual cases of pupils or teachers provides a depth that is impossible with any other method. A case study requires careful selection of subjects who are reasonably representative of the population used for the group research. Case studies usually encompass such areas as the subject's demographic data, behaviours, attitudes and their responses to specific creative learning stimuli, so as to provide an in-depth narrative.

This method has two specific purposes in research on creative learn-ing:

☐ it helps to isolate critical variables for subsequent larger-scale studies which may involve broad investigations or experimental approaches; and

☐ it enhances the interpretation of other qualitative and quan-titative data with examples that illustrate the effects of specific teaching or learning in relation to creativity.

9. *Audiotapes and videotapes.* If the research budget permits, the best way to collect data is to use audio or videotapes of classroom interactions for the analysis of pupil and teacher behaviours. Some researchers hesitate to use these devices because they fear that the intrusion could affect pupils' and teachers' responses. In fact, both teachers and pupils quickly adapt to the presence of recording equipment, if it does not intrude on classroom interaction (Burton and Bartlett, 2005).

However, there is a significant resource issue, since verbal and non-verbal data from the recordings must be transcribed. The PRAXIS III system for analysis of teacher behaviours is an example of a research-based and tested method for analysing video-recorded classroom interaction. It uses nineteen specific criteria in four behavioural domains, as developed by the Educational Testing Service in New Jersey (1994). NVivo is a similar analytical method used in the UK. An alternative to using audiotapes and videotapes is the systematic analysis of classroom photographs taken of pupils or teachers when they are involved in some creative learning activity (see also Atlas-Ti www.atlasti.com and its application in Jeffrey, 2006 for ways in which a qualitative computer software programme was used by the researchers involved in a European comparative study of creative teaching and learning).

10. *Surveys.* The written survey is an excellent means to research attitudes and beliefs. This technique benefits from pilot testing to ensure that the wording of survey items is unambiguous and valid. It is also important to give adequate time for a meaningful response from pupils. Many models of surveys exist, and guidelines for their careful development can be found in many texts on educational or social science research. Surveys on younger pupils can ask them to indicate their choices for each item by circling a smiling, neutral or frowning face.

11. *Research subjects' self-reports.* Reports by pupils about how they believe their own creative thinking has changed since the inception of some kind of intervention or in which they reflect back on how they carried out some creative task (meta-cognition) are crucial. With pupils aged 8 and over, it is worth asking them to complete sentences such as, 'When I have a problem to which I don't know the solution, I now...', as a means of investigating any changes in their problem-solving approaches.

Critical factors

Before embarking on a selection of methods the practitioner-researcher should consider the following factors:

- Before beginning formal data-collection or data analysis, the researcher needs to maintain a journal of observational notes in which she or he makes a record of informal findings that may lend themselves to more formal study and analysis. Some writers have called this activity 'hanging around' (Hubbard and Power, 1999), because it involves unobtrusively standing to one side and simply watching and notating. From these notes useful research designs may evolve.

- Since teacher and pupil behaviours frequently interact, we must examine both when carrying out research on creative learning.

- We must constantly test and re-test our hypotheses in order to ensure that we do not become bound by limited orientations or unproven findings.

- We must bear in mind that creativity is culturally specific, which means that instruments must be retested in relation to their validity and reliability for different cultural contexts (Symposium, 2005). The researcher also needs to be aware of their own cultural lens, since they are viewing data from their own perspective. In many countries, school populations are widely multicultural, so this consideration is essential for credible research. One idea is for teams of researchers who represent possible cultural traditions to collaborate in order to avoid possible cultural bias.

- Above all, we must implement triangulation in such research – the deliberate use of a variety of techniques in order to have multiple avenues for data collection and interpretation. This will produce well-supported conclusions.

Who should the practitioner researchers be?

At least three constituencies may fill this function:

- with appropriate training and collaboration, the classroom teacher may play a vital role in conceiving and conducting the research

- university-based professional researchers trained in research methodologies can bring unique skills and experience to the research enterprise.

■ The pupils themselves as learners can inform research in three ways: as research subjects they may reflect upon and record how their own creative acts evolved; by conducting their own data collection and analysis as part of a creative project, they can apply creativity to learner-based research; and they may be valuable research partners in interpreting the data collected by the adult researchers.

Summary

There is an exciting variety of choices for researchers in the field of creative learning. Although some of the methods described in this chapter go well beyond traditional educational research, these are not the only options available. Let us use our own creativity to develop further techniques and combinations of methods, providing an enhanced view of the excitement of creative learning.

On a final note, a highly recommended read is Hubbard and Power's *Living the questions: A guide for teacher researchers* (1999). This book is a manual for the practitioner-researcher and emphasises qualitative and classroom-based investigative methods.

References

Burnard, P (2006) Provocations in creativity research. In L Bresler (ed) *International Handbook of Research in Arts Education*. Dordrecht: Springer, p2003-2015

Burton, D and Bartlett, S (2005) *Practitioner research for teachers*. London: Paul Chapman Publishing

Creswell, J (2003) *Research design: qualitative, quantitative and mixed methods approaches*. London: Sage

Crotty, M (2005) *The foundations of social research: meaning and perspective in the research process*. London: Sage

Educational Testing Service (1994) *PRAXIS III: A teacher performance system*. Princeton, New Jersey: Educational Testing Service

Greene, S and Hogan, D (2005) (eds) *Researching children's experience: Approaches and methods*. London: Sage

Hammersley, M. (1992) Some reflections on ethnography and validity. *Qualitative Studies in Education*, 5 (3) p193-203

Hubbard, R and Power, B (1999) *Living the questions: A guide for teacher-researchers*. York, Maine: Stenhouse Publishers

Jeffrey, B (2005) *Documenting creative learning: A meaning-making objective*. Presentation at the British Education Research Association Conference, September 2005, Glamorgan

Jeffrey, B (2006) Creative teaching and learning: towards a common discourse and practice. *Cambridge Journal of Education* 36(3) p399-415

Martin, D, Craft, A, and Zhang, N (2001) The impact of cognitive strategy instruction on deaf learners: An international comparative study. *American Annals of the Deaf*, 146(4) p366-378.

Raven, J C (1959) *Standard progressive matrices.* New York: Psychological Corporation

Symposium on Documenting Creative Learning (2005) *Discussion summaries.* Cambridge University, England, April 2005

Winocur, S L (1991) Classroom observation checklist. In A Costa (ed), *Developing minds.* Alexandria, VA: Association for Supervision and Curriculum Development, p 386-388

PART TWO
INTRODUCTION
How does creative learning happen?

Pamela Burnard, Teresa Cremin, Anna Craft

This volume seeks to exemplify what is involved when creative learning happens. Another imperative is to examine what mitigates against the development of creativity in the curriculum. There is contemporary interest in the relationship between development and learning, between theoretical positions and empirical findings. This is particularly so for those who are committed to the domain free, domain specific, individual disciplinary-focused and interdisciplinary views of creative learning, and the perceived impact of creativity on learning and of learning on creativity. All these influence interpretations of how creative learning happens.

The range of perspectives featured in Part Two illustrates the importance of, and our commitment to, evidence-based research. Authors working in diverse cultures celebrate the richness and the range of ways in which children can engage in and interact with creative learning. It presents theory, both cutting edge and classic, in an accessible way for readers by providing a survey and synthesis of the available literature from the UK, North America and the Far East, and by reference to a range of empirical studies.

For Craft, Cremin, Burnard and Chappell, in the UK where there is a much greater emphasis on explicit policy making to encourage creative learning, evidence is drawn from the close-up focus on children's questioning with 'possibility thinking' at the heart of creativity. This is characterised by children's self-determination and imagination, as shown in actions flowing from question posing. For Churchill Dower creative learning is shown in practice, reflecting four elements: artist-teacher collaboration, environment, embedded creative learning practice and parental involvement. In the context of dance education, Chappell argues that creative learning happens at the inter-face of immersion, imagination, idea-generation and originality, and that the specific knowledge of the domain is vital to the ways this interface is mani-fested in children's behaviours.

Wong shows how deeply cultural values influence the theory and practice of creative learning. This chapter puts the cultural focus on teachers and peda-gogical strategies for fostering children's creative and critical thinking. In contrast, Smyth illustrates how creative learning involves various dimensions of imagination by her documentation of children's drawings. Here we see creative learning embodied in the auditory, kinaesthetic, emotional and visual elements of her AKTEV model.

The promotion of creative learning as something which can be both made explicit and strongly fostered through social and collaborative processes is put forward by Mardell, Otami and Turner. These authors feature research-into-practice emanating from an innovative laboratory school at Tufts University (USA). This is based on the practice of Reggio Emilia pre-schools in Northern Italy, where careful written, pictorial and audio documentation is used as a tool for tracking each child's learning journey. They explore depths of creative learning fostered through a lens of metacognition.

The need for the professional development of teachers to feature heavily in the push to raise educational standards and to identify culturally what characterises creative learning practices is common to all the chapters. It is agreed that all children are capable of creative achievements in some areas of activity provided the conditions are right and they have acquired the relevant knowledge and skills. It is also agreed that the significance of creative teach-ing and its impact at multiple levels is well established.

Key differences between the chapters arise from the kinds of evidence pro-vided and the extent to which creative learning is emphasised as being mani-fest at individual, group or cultural levels. The authors agree that creative learning is a crucial element of education and that the challenge is to provide opportunities that enable it to happen and make explicit the cultural assumptions that underpin these opportunities.

8

Possibility thinking with children in England aged 3-7

Anna Craft, Teresa Cremin, Pamela Burnard,
Kerry Chappell

Creative learning and possibility thinking

In recent years creative learning has been explored by researchers across Europe (Jeffrey, 2005). Analysis emerging from empirical work suggests that the creative in creative learning signals involvement of pupils in 'being innovative, experimental and inventive' (*ibid*), and the learning signifies that pupils 'engage in aspects of ...intellectual enquiry'. The authors suggest that within this process of intellectual enquiry, a significant dimension is around 'possibility thinking and engagement with problems' (*ibid*).

In England, the early 21st century saw energy invested in conceptualising and developing both learning and pedagogy, in schools and elsewhere, through a range of organisations including Creative Partnerships (Creative Partnerships, 2007), National College for School Leadership (NCSL, 2004) and the Qualifications and Curriculum Authority (QCA 2005a, 2005b), funded through a variety of government departments. Much of this work has been influenced by the statement proposed by the National Advisory Committee on Creative and Cultural Education, that creativity is 'imaginative activity fashioned so as to produce outcomes that are original and of value' (NACCCE, 1999, p29). It led to the development of a policy framework for creativity by the QCA (2005a, 2005b), one aspect of which focused on a conceptualisation of imaginative activity, what NACCCE saw as being at the heart of creativity – which is where this study begins.

The study reported in this chapter draws on a body of literature which posits the notion of possibility thinking being at the heart of creativity in education (Craft, 2000, 2001; Jeffrey and Craft, 2004). Possibility thinking is construed as being at the core of creativity, whether individual or collective (Craft, 2001 and 2007). At its most fundamental, it involves the posing, in multiple ways, of the question 'What if?' and therefore involves the shift from 'what is this and what does it do?' to 'What can I do with this?'. Implicit within it, is what the CLASP team call 'engagement with problems' (Jeffrey, 2005). It involves finding and honing problems as well as solving them, a distinction explored through studies in primary classrooms (Jeffrey, 2005; Jeffrey and Craft, 2004).

Possibility thinking may be vital to 'big c' creativity. However the focus of our work has been on 'little c creativity', at the other end of the spectrum. This concern with little c creativity occurs in an English cultural context where in 1999 the NACCCE Report advocated that educators should adopt a democratic approach, arguing that all can be creative, not just the highly talented, domain-shifting, few.

Concrete proposals in that report led to policy development (QCA 2005a, 2005b, DfES, 2003, 2004a, 2004b). From the early 2000s, increasing attention was paid to creativity in the curriculum. The introduction of Creative Development for 3-5 year olds in 2000 and the codifying of creative thinking skills in the national curriculum for 5-16 year olds, was followed from 2005 by at least two key curriculum reviews. In late 2005 and early 2006 the Roberts review of creativity and the economy (Roberts, 2006), which was responded to by the government (DCMS, 2006), further focused policy attention on creativity in all phases of education from the early years through to higher education.

Common to all these developments is the commitment to little c creativity – everyday, 'lifewide' creativity as well as the creativity inherent within domains studied as subjects in schools (Craft, 2000, 2001, 2002). Whilst possibility thinking may be just as relevant to adults as it is to children, this chapter discusses what we know about the questioning core of children's possibility thinking.

An empirical study of possibility thinking

The Possibility Thinking team sought to identify and document what characterises possibility thinking in creative learning for children aged 3-7. In addition, we aimed to develop innovative methodological ways of identifying and documenting what constitutes possibility thinking in the learning experiences of young children, and how teachers foster it as an aspect of creativity (Burnard *et al*, 2006).

The study, ongoing at the time of writing, commenced in October 2004. We adopted a case study approach, working with three core teachers over time using multiple sources of data to develop understanding of each site: an early childhood centre in London, an infant school in South East England, and a primary school in the Midlands. The teachers formed part of the research team, working collaboratively with the four researchers based in three universities. The teachers had been featured in video material by QCA as creative practitioners. Data sources included interviews, participant and non-participant observation, video material (QCA's, plus additional material collected specially), and whole group data surgery sessions using video stimulated review and other techniques.

Naturalistic collaborative enquiry approaches encouraging careful reflection on and reconstruction of practice sat alongside observation and systematic event recording. The study sought to enrich the thinking and approaches of practitioners and researchers through systematic and reflective documentation (Stenhouse, 1975).

The analytical approach was deductive-inductive. We worked deductively in using the existing Possibility Thinking framework (Craft, 2000) and the QCA framework (2005a, 2005b), looking for evidence of the key factors of possibility thinking and the presumed relationships between them from the data. We also worked inductively, identifying emergent themes and categories. In this way we aimed to ground and support our theory-building, benefiting from the focusing and bounding function of a conceptual framework whilst also enabling new concepts to emerge (Glaser and Strauss, 1967, Strauss and Corbin, 1998).

Our focus shifted over time through two stages. In Stage 1 we fleshed out the operational elements of possibility thinking and pedagogy, and in Stage 2 we carried out a fine-grained analysis of children's questions.

Operational elements of possibility thinking and pedagogy

Stage 1 resulted in the identification of close interplay between children and adults in fostering possibility thinking with children aged 3 – 7 (Burnard *et al*, 2006, Cremin *et al*, 2006). The study involved working closely with staff in the three separate settings to investigate both their pedagogic practices and children's learning. The research team identified a number of distinct but interlinked core features of children's and teachers' engagement which are valued and fostered in each setting, in an enabling environment, as follows:

■ **Posing questions** – children's questions; both those posed aloud, and others, implied through actions, were documented through close observation of behaviours and deep knowledge of each individual. Questions were treated with interest and respect. Posing questions often involved imaginative playful thinking with children in an 'as if' space.

■ **Play** – children were encouraged to play over extended periods, allowing ideas to develop and combine. Children travelled far in play, highly motivated by their interests and development of knowledge. They were often highly engaged, serious in their playfulness, engaging closely with one another, imagining scenes, encountering and solving diverse problems. Their play reflected what Sylva *et al* (1986) describe as high cognitive challenge.

■ **Immersion** – the children were deeply immersed in a loving environment in each classroom. The importance of providing love and support is highlighted by Bruce (2004), also by writers from the psychoanalytic tradition (Winnicott, 1971; Freud, 1914). The provision of a caring, positive, benign environment was notable. Yet in each case overt cognitive challenge was present, deepening imagination.

■ **Innovation** – children made strong and playful connections between ideas. Adults working with them closely observed changes in each child's thinking and probed growing understandings, offering well-chosen provocations to stimulate the children's ability to make connections.

■ **Being imaginative** – children engaged extensively in imagining what might be, inventing imaginary worlds. They were decision makers on the feasibility of ideas, the content of learning tasks and ways of conducting them.

■ **Self-determination and risk-taking** – children's deep involvement was encouraged, as was risk taking. They worked in safe, secure, supportive environments, were expected to exercise independence in making decisions and their contributions were valued. Adults encouraged learning from experience as both empowering and generative, enabling children to move with confidence into original and creative spaces.

Stage 1 highlighted the significance of the enabling context. Each site encouraged playfulness in children and teachers, encouraging self-confidence

Figure 8.1: Adults' approaches to Possibility Thinking reproduced from Cremin, T., Burnard, P., Craft, A. (2006), Pedagogy and possibility thinking in the early years, *Thinking Skills and Creativity* Vol.1, Issue 2, Autumn 2006, pp108-119

and self-esteem. Adults placed value on children's agency, motivation and engagement. High engagement is vital to quality learning in the early years (Laevers, 1993, Pascal and Bertram, 1997). Teachers offered children time and space to have ideas and to see them through. They stepped back, so that children's activity led the pedagogy (see Figure 8.1).

Stage 1 also illustrated 'agentive' learning environments, i.e. those fostering agency, and supporting children's questioning (Burnard *et al*, 2006). It led us to explore questions more closely in Stage 2, working with video based material from the 4-5 year-olds' and the 5-7 year-olds' classroom. The activity record (Werner, 1992, Werner and Shoepfle, 1987) was adopted to document and explain children's actions and engagement. Micro analysis developed, from detailed transcription of talk and activity by specific children who were engaged in immersed activity. We hoped that detailed documentation of verbal and non-verbal questioning would clearly demonstrate how the questioning core of possibility thinking is manifest in children's classroom activity.

Children's questions in possibility thinking

Discussion of these is necessarily provisional, since, at the time of writing, Stage 2 analysis is still under way, with multiple video-recorded episodes being micro-analysed by a university-based researcher. Peer checking was adopted through triangulated analysis for selected episodes. We distinguished between question posing and question responding, both verbal and non-verbal.

In exploring question posing, children asked three different types of questions:

- Leading questions – the overall questions
- Service questions – those generated to help to answer the leading question
- Follow through questions – which are often to do with practicalities such as negotiating the use of resources.

Within each category, questions are classified on a spectrum from broad to narrow relating to inherent possibility.

In our exploration of question answering, we found the following responses: testing, predicting, undoing, accepting, rejecting, evaluating, compensating, completing and repeating.

The analysis provided strong evidence of the significance of some operational elements of possibility thinking confirmed in Stage 1:

- **Being imaginative** – children exercised imagination in all episodes, in play with objects, ideas and each other, going beyond 'as if' thinking – which is talking about or using an object as if it represents something else – to include being aware of unconventionality, making unusual interpretations, and stepping beyond the obvious.

- **Self-determination** – this was also evidenced in all episodes, and was more obvious where children had greater opportunities for child-initiated, or self-directed, activity; in our data, the older children worked within increasingly tight task structures.

- **Action/intention** – children in these micro-episodes demonstrated powerful intentionality and action flowing from this, perhaps reflecting how far they are encouraged to be self-determined. Interestingly early analysis suggests that the older children demonstrate stronger action/intention than the younger children – despite self-determination being slightly less prominent.

In so far as the enabling context of play and immersion is assumed by the nature of the episodes recorded, it has been inactive in the analysis; along with risk taking, development and innovation; further re-analysis is ongoing to consider these to further define each and to explore their relationship to the core operational features of possibility thinking.

Implications

In terms of classroom practice, our study highlights the significance of a warm and encouraging ethos, and the dilemma of balancing structure and freedom, adult- and child- initiated learning, in classrooms. Too much structure or adult-determination can restrict children's self-determination and capacity to develop their own ideas. On the other hand total freedom may confuse, and may not enable a child to reach beyond themselves as far as they might. Finding the right balance is challenging. The practitioners' skills in noticing how children respond and engage, and their capacity to document and reflect on what was happening and adjust their pedagogy accordingly, was remarkable. From a standpoint of deep respect, noticing the multiple and multi-modal questions which children pose and respond to, is a vital part of this reflective cycle. The co-participative, learner-inclusive approaches we witnessed handed control over the investigation of knowledge back to the child (Jeffrey and Craft, 2004). Children were offered the opportunity and authority to be innovative, and for their experiences, imagination and evaluation to be valued (Jeffrey, 2001). Our study demonstrates how such practices show deep involvement and high inclusion.

Reflective practice, in which teachers stand back, to consider what children are telling them through their engagement in the classroom, is integral to achieving this. It also involves documenting these moments in some way, as a mental snapshot, as actual still or moving images, as notes, or in special circumstances as recordings which may be played back later. Documentation enables us to note and respond to pertinent events, responses and comments. It means reflecting on what we learn from both standing back and documenting, in order to appropriately support and stimulate their learning.

Standing back means being deeply engaged with children's learning, responsive to their ideas, engaging in what Schon (1987) called reflection-in-action. It often means working with others, to share perspectives on what is being observed. In our study, classroom teachers worked with university researchers, but in other contexts documenting learning can be done by children as well as adults, and the results shared in discussion in order to take next appropriate next steps in learning. It is important to consider what is done with documentation, and how it might form part of a shared record. Strategies often used include post-it notes and other documentation on wall space, learning logs or portfolios, and home-school records. The key point is that in each case multiple ownership is encouraged, in making and using a record of creative learning. Working with other adults also goes some way towards starting a conversation which might reveal perspectives on the value and purposes of creativity, and the purposes of it, both among staff and also between practitioners and parents.

Summing up

It appears that in reinforcing children's capabilities as confident explorers, meaning makers and decision makers, possibility thinking builds their resilience and confidence. Vital to creative learning, the potential for developing reflective practice with children aged 3-11 to encourage and nurture possibility thinking, seems unquestionable.

Thanks are due to Susanne Jasilek, and Anne Meredith, both Consultant Researchers to the Open University, also Bernadette Duffy and Ruth Hanson, Thomas Coram Early Childhood Centre, London, Jean Keene and Lindsay Haynes, Cunningham Hill Infant School, Hertfordshire, Dawn Burns, Hackleton Primary School, Northamptonshire.

References

Bruce, T (2004) *Cultivating Creativity in Babies, Toddlers and Young Children.* London: Hodder and Stoughton Educational

Burnard, P, Craft, A and Grainger, T *et al* (2006) Possibility Thinking, *International Journal of Early Years Education*, 14 (3) p243-262

Craft, A (2000) *Creativity Across the Primary Curriculum.* London: Routledge

Craft, A (2001) Little c Creativity. In A Craft, B Jeffrey, M Leibling (eds) *Creativity in Education*, London: Continuum

Craft, A (2002) *Creativity and Early Years Education.* London: Continuum

Craft, A and Jeffrey, B (2004) Learner inclusiveness for creative learning. *Education 3-13*, 32 (2)

Craft, A (2007) Creativity and Early Years Settings. In A Paige-Smith and A Craft (eds) *Reflecting on Practice: Exploring Issues in Early Years Education and Care.* Buckingham: Open University Press

Creative Partnerships (2007) Website: http://www.creative-partnerships.com/ (April 2007)

Cremin, T, Burnard, P, Craft, A (2006) Pedagogy and possibility thinking in the early years, *International Journal of Thinking Skills and Creativity* 1(2) p108-119

Department for Culture, Media and Sport (2006) *Government Response to Paul Roberts' Report on Nurturing Creativity in Young People.* London DCMS

Department for Education and Skills (2003) *Excellence and Enjoyment,* London: HMSO

Department for Education and Skills (2004a) *Every Child Matters: Change for Children in Schools.* London: HMSO

Department for Education and Skills (2004b) *Excellence and Enjoyment: learning and teaching in the primary years.* London: HMSO

Freud, S (1914) *On the Psychopathology of Everyday Life*, New York: Macmillan (original German publication, 1904)

Glaser, B and Strauss, A (1967) *The discovery of grounded theory: strategies for qualitative research.* Chicago: Aldine

Jeffrey, B (2005) Final Report of the Creative Learning and Student Perspectives Research Project (CLASP), A European Commission Funded project through the Socrates Programme, Action 6.1, Number 2002 – 4682/002 – 001. SO2 – 61OBGE. Milton Keynes: http://clasp.open.ac.uk

Jeffrey, B and Craft, A (2004) Teaching Creatively and Teaching for Creativity: distinctions and relationships, *Educational Studies* 30, No.1, March 2004 (pages 77-87)

Laevers, F (1993) Deep Level Learning – An Exemplary Application on the Area of Physical Knowledge. *European Early Childhood Education Research Journal* 1(1) p53-68

National Advisory Committee on Creative and Cultural Education (NACCCE) (1999) *All Our Futures: Creativity, Culture and Education.* London: Department for Education and Employment

National College for School Leadership (2004) *Developing Creativity in the Primary School.* Nottingham: NCSL

Pascal, C and Bertram, A (eds) (1997) *Effective Early Learning: Case Studies of Improvement.* London: Hodder and Stoughton

Qualifications and Curriculum Authority (QCA) (2005a) *Creativity: Find it, promote – Promoting pupils' creative thinking and behaviour across the curriculum at key stages 1, 2 and 3 – practical materials for schools*, London: Qualifications and Curriculum Authority

Qualifications and Curriculum Authority (QCA) (2005b) website: http://www.ncaction.org.uk/creativity/about.htm Last accessed 19th April 2007

Roberts, P (2006) *Nurturing Creativity in Young People. A Report to Government to Inform Future Policy.* London: Department for Culture, Media and Sport

Schon D (1987) *Educating the Reflective Practitioner.* Josey Bass, San Francisco

Stenhouse, L (1975) *An introduction to curriculum research and development.* London: Heinemann

Strauss, A L and Corbin, J M (1998) *Basics of qualitative research: techniques and procedures for developing grounded theory* (2nd edn) (Newbury Park CA Sage).

Sylva, K, Roy, C, Painter, M (1986) *Childwatching and Playgroup and Nursery School,* Oxford: Blackwell

Werner, O (1992) How to record activities. *Cultural Anthropology Methods Newsletter* 4(2) p1-3

Werner, O and Schoepfle, G M (1987) *Systematic fieldwork, vol.1: Foundations of ethnography and interviewing* (Newbury Park CA Sage)

Winnicott, D (1971) *Playing and Reality.* Harmondsworth: Penguin

9

Fostering creative learning for 3-5 year olds in four international settings

Ruth Churchill Dower

Children have a right to experience creative learning opportunities to enable them to have healthy learning journeys. As adults, educators, creative practitioners or carers, we can make this happen by providing a creative learning experience which should be as holistic, high quality, well planned, appropriate and inclusive a creative learning experience as possible.

The evidence set out in this chapter outlines how this can be achieved and asserts that there are clear factors that foster creative thinking and learning, particularly in primary and nursery settings. It also demonstrates that these factors are closely related across international cultural and geographical divides.

In November 2003, Arts Council England funded a programme of research into three international models of creative practice in early years education settings. The aim was to identify characteristics of effective creative learning in settings beyond the UK, particularly focusing on collaborative approaches between artists and nursery professionals, in order to influence the work of arts and early years' educators in the UK. The research was gathered intensively over a period of six months using desk and web-based research to identify a wide range of potential projects. Scoping questionnaires were sent to ascertain the extent and approaches to creative learning with under 5s in twenty three countries: four case studies were chosen and the participants interviewed extensively by telephone, email and during face to face observational visits. The evidence and findings were gathered into a report which was published by Arts Council England, disseminated across the *earlyarts* networks (www.earlyarts.co.uk), and presented at the national early years and creativity conference, New Worlds, at West Yorkshire Playhouse in 2004.

The findings emphasised the values of creative practice in children's learning in terms of gaining confidence, helping to express and communicate feelings, thoughts, and ideas, developing a sense of identity and individuality, and learning new skills (Perkins, 1998). Equally important benefits were demonstrated for parents, nursery staff, child carers, educationalists and arts practitioners in approaching learning through creative means. These included helping to identify children's strong and weak points, exploring new techniques and skills, language and literature development, breaking down social barriers in the home, empowering effective teaching, and giving children a voice (Clark *et al*, 2003).

This research highlights the work of four key players who have demonstrated some of the most progressive practice across Europe over the last thirty years: Théâtre de la Guimbarde (Charleroi, Belgium), La Baracca Theatre (Bologna, Italy), Balabik Dance Company (Limoges, France), and Bradford County Regional Arts Council (Pennsylvania, US). It attempts to highlight the strategies they employ for empowering creative learning not just within children from the earliest age, but also within their parents, carers and workers.

Théâtre de la Guimbarde's work started in 1973 during an important time of decentralisation of the government in France and Belgium. It began as a combination of a political community arts movement dedicated to tackling social justice issues, and a network of writers and directors from both the voluntary and professional communities whose work is entirely influenced by, and reflective of, the community they try to support. Their recent work has been particularly inspired by very young children, helping them to explore and make sense of their place in the world.

At the same time, over 1000 miles south in Bologna, a company of fifty people, La Baracca, have been tackling similar issues. Back in 1976, La Baracca started as a children's theatre company by Roberto and Valeria Frabetti, recognising the increasing importance of building creative learning and play environments with children both within and outside of the formal education system. They believe that the competencies required for survival and success in life are the same as those needed in the theatre, so their theatre work is directly informed by the children creating it as their learning develops.

In a similar way, Balabik Dance Theatre Company has been running peda-gogic workshops in crèches, kindergartens and nursery schools for fifteen years. Through movement or dance, they build strategies or 'toolkits' for shared creative learning between children and their parents, trying to avoid creating negative expectations of learning behaviours. They aim to develop an understanding of the complexity of children's cognitive, social and emotional learning and an ability to respond positively to children's indivi-dual learning needs.

The same broad impact is achieved by the Bradford County Regional Arts Council (BCRAC) based in Pennsylvania, USA, working across seven counties covering huge pockets of social and economic deprivation, in contexts where cycles of violence and abuse are common. BCRAC works in partnership with families to tackle issues head on through creative learning programmes in order to break cycles for future generations.

Research from all the case studies demonstrated that four key approaches are needed for creative learning to have a meaningful and long term impact on the lives of young children. These approaches are not exhaustive and are limited by the scope and extent of the research itself; however, they do concur with factors evidenced through other more formal studies (Bamford, 2005; Burke, 2005; Deasy and Stevenson, 2005; Harland *et al*, 2005) and so provide a fundamental framework for effective creative learning to take place.

Collaboration

All the case studies cited the importance of artists working collaboratively with teachers to explore and meet children's learning needs with fresh eyes. In designing their theatre performances, both La Baracca and La Guimbarde used an experiential learning approach. This involved spending a long time with young children to get to know them and the people, memories, environ-ments and situations that influenced them, so they could rigorously measure the long-term impact of their creative approaches on the children's learning. They learned how to communicate without being invasive and how to res-pond most effectively to the children's learning styles, their rhythms of life and their emotional make-up. They learned how to see life through young children's eyes, using all their senses as if for the first time, and as if every moment was real and important for them, in order to gain insight into the children's lives and to achieve the most suitable learning environment possible for them.

BCRAC have similarly developed a five year programme of artists' residencies in primary schools, operating in particularly hard to reach, often uncreative environments. BCRAC's artists and teachers frequently referred to the need to learn each others' languages as an important process in both the breaking down of perceived fears and prejudices, and the building up of confidence in working together. Effective collaborations acknowledged that each was an expert in their own field, including the children who are experts at being children.

> We should not be in the business of telling them how to 'do' creative learning *per se* but facilitating their ability to express who they are better. The essence of working as an artist with a young child is to find that child's potential, then build the environment around that potential in order to let that child shine. (Rand Whipple, BCRAC Theatre Artist, 2003)

This democratic practice enabled points of partnership with opportunities for each other's skills and knowledge to be significantly complemented and enhanced. As such, artists and teachers were able to build a legacy of creative learning methodologies where teachers continued to implement their own creative ideas with relative confidence once the residencies were finished.

That is not to say that the artists' role was superseded. Aside from their contribution of creative skills and knowledge, the artists brought new ways of looking at life and learning which facilitated communication around issues not always obvious to those trained to work within an educational framework (Belloli and Woolf, 2005; Clarke, Griffiths and Taylor, 2003).

Environment

Our case studies demonstrated a high level of engagement in creative learning when participants felt inspired, safe and confident enough. Having arts skills, although useful, may not be pre-requisite to creative learning, thinking or doing, but having the right environment is (Edwards, Pope and Springate, 1995).

> The early learning environment should be a safe space to explore and learn with enough time to facilitate creativity, the right people to support the process who can think laterally, and resources which are fit for the purpose. The ethos of such space should be process oriented rather than product driven, and be flexible enough to encourage risk taking by both adults and children. The ultimate aim should be to harness a natural learning space which can happen anywhere at any time. *Imagination for Life and Learning, an Early Years and Creativity Development Plan* (Churchill Dower, 2005)

Théâtre de la Guimbarde's work takes place within a highly institutionalised context in Belgian crèches; nursery nurses wear uniforms and work to strict routines. Since the whole nursery care system is funded by the ministry of health, it has an extremely health oriented focus. There is a lack of any pedagogic structure in the day except for eating, sleeping and playing and the environment is generally not one which inspires or fosters opportunities for creative learning.

La Guimbarde's actors focus much of their initial work on re-creating an environment which reflects the identities, cultures and influences of both children and staff outside of the setting. This recreation involves a variety of creative resources as necessary, using silks and soft materials, natural outdoor materials, music and sounds, and sensual materials such as feathers and water. The intention is to help to build an environment which reflects a positive sense of self, and therefore helps to engage with and stimulate a positive learning experience.

Balabik dancers also take a holistic environmental approach, understanding the importance of creating both physically and emotionally secure spaces for children and staff before exploring creative approaches to learning outside their learnt regimes (Belloli and Woolf, 2005; Duffy, 1998). In creating positive learning environments, both companies try to use as many available and natural physical, musical, or kinaesthetic resources as possible so that the environment can be initiated or re-created at any time by staff and the creative work continued.

> If we get the environment right to start with, then they learn to watch and listen to the children's responses, to become less forceful and more respectful of them as individuals with individual desires and learning needs. It is a method based on emotional and physical responses to situations and environments rather than intellectual ones, and requires a lot of reflection and time to develop a deeper understanding of themselves and their children. It results in a tremendous relationship built on trust, honesty and respect rather than one where everyone has to fit the system regardless of individual needs or characteristics. (Noelle Dehousse, Director, Balabik, 2003)

Both Balabik and La Guimbarde quoted instances of nursery managers displaying initial hostility to this approach, fearing anarchy and a complete lack of regard for the rules and guidelines of their existing environment. However, the opposite was often the result with children developing an even better regard for the adults and for themselves, as their relationship became centred around trust, exploration, risk taking and openness. In these environments, children and staff saw themselves from different perspectives, learning new ways of offering and receiving meaningful communications, leading to a higher level of engagement with their own and each other's learning.

Embedded practice

Children are constantly growing and changing, seeking new challenges and new learning. The impact of this creative practice on their lives is not always immediately evident and needs to be measured and analysed over a much longer period of time, in synergy with their growth.

Whilst short term arts workshops and performances have an important part to play in the introduction to and acceptance of creative practices, they are unlikely to achieve real lasting effects. Work which is meaningful to children should be based on their interests, desires and needs, all of which takes time to understand and to build up the trust which allows for spontaneous interaction (Clarke *et al*, 2003).

This long term approach to work offers opportunities to build skills and experiences which are tailored to the needs of the children, staff and environment, within which they will continue to work once the artist has left. In addition, the different languages of educational and creative practices can be shared, learned and in time become mutually integrated (Perkins, 1998).

In order to extend the possibilities of the children's creative learning experience, both La Guimbarde and La Barracca worked for long periods with nursery teachers to help them understand and take pleasure in the spontaneity of creative play. In doing so, they helped to break the habits of routines and encourage an ongoing state of discovery. Embedding creative practice within their daily work helped staff to develop a sense of purpose around challenging issues, giving them the confidence and skills in creative learning to approach these situations from different angles, reducing the amount of isolation or lack of control felt in their work.

However, this has been no easy task. In Belgium particularly, a common issue kept occurring – nursery teachers felt unable to think 'outside the box', constrained by any combination of lack of experience, age, education, status, self-esteem, ability to articulate themselves, or confidence. Théâtre de la Guimbarde recognised the need for a simultaneous top-down intervention so that nurseries without such enlightened staff might still feel they had permission to try out, and even embed, more creative methods. They worked in partnership with the education ministry to investigate the impact of creative interventions on raising standards in early education, and are now working with training providers to design creative practices within the initial training of nursery teachers.

To encourage embedded creative learning practices within nurseries, since 1990 La Baracca have pioneered the growth of a summer laboratory for *puericultrici* (Italian nursery nurses trained to degree level) to explore environments which would stimulate young children's creative thinking and learning, reflect on their discoveries, and teach each other the creative skills they were learning. Participants are now leading peer-to-peer skills training within the nurseries on a daily basis. This has had a profound impact on the validity, longevity and acceptance of creative practice within the nursery setting. There are now over one hundred trained *puericultrici* using methodologies which foster creative approaches to learning within their nurseries. The laboratory programme is now expanding across Europe as the *puericultrici* work in nurseries across Spain, France, Belgium and in England.

> Roberto Frabetti can do a workshop for the *puericultrici* but he is a professional [actor/director], they are not, so the simple presence of them in nursery has much more impact than La Baracca actors. They are the same as other *puericultrici*, they are accepted more easily and without fear and they have the knowledge of both the children's and *puericultrici* needs, and so on. This is how they transfer the belief in creative learning further afield; it's not just a one-off but very much a part of their culture. (Valeria Frabetti, Director, La Baracca, 2003)

Parental involvement

Time is also required to involve parents and carers in the process, from planning right through to delivery, so that they experience, understand, enjoy and continue the creative learning at home. Balabik dancers commented on the effectiveness of a joint creative learning process in breaking the habit of routines, and in engaging a state of ongoing spontaneity and discovery. This collaborative approach had the powerful effect of reawakening both parents and nursery teachers to the potential of their children, and challenging prejudices they might have held as to what was possible. (Belloli and Woolf, 2005).

In one example, during a workshop, the children invited their parents and grandparents, who had never danced before, to participate in a dance session. The parents and grandparents presumed such a session would be simple. As the children led the adults through relaxation and other exercises, the parents realised how difficult and complex it was, and how much their children had learned. This was especially poignant for parents whose children had displayed what had been identified as behavioural or learning disabilities: they saw them focused, participating, and learning in a way they had not before witnessed in either their home or school environments. They witnessed their children concentrating for long periods of time without crying, moving, fidgeting, or causing disruptions, participating in an imaginative, motivated and creative way and working constructively with each other (Oagliari and Guidici, 2001).

Conclusion

Through the creative learning approaches of arts practitioners working collaboratively with teachers, engaging parents, embedding practice and designing environments which enable children's potential to flourish, this investigation revealed a series of common skills, attitudes and environments which provided a framework for successful creative learning. These four factors can together provide a flexible and creative approach to learning which greatly enhances the child's social, cultural, educational and cognitive faculties. In all examples, the design of the creative learning processes was influenced by the desires, environments and cultures of the learners, not by a formal approach to curriculum delivery. Yet, in spite of the bottom-up learner directed approach, all four approaches also resulted in the successful delivery of curriculum requirements for that country.

References

Bamford, A (2006) *The WOW Factor – Global research compendium on the impact of the arts in education*. Waxmann

Belloli, J and Woolf, F (2005) *Reflect and Review, The arts and creativity in early years*. Arts Council England

Burke K (2005) *Creativity Action Research Awards: a critical evaluation*. Leeds University and CAPE UK

Churchill Dower, R (2005) *Imagination for Life and Learning, an Early Years and Creativity Development Plan*, Arts Council England

Clark, J Griffiths, C and Taylor H (2003) *Feeding The Mind, Valuing the arts in the development of young children*. Arts Council England, North East

Deasy R J and Stevenson L (2005) *Third Space: When Learning Matters*. Washington DC: Arts Education Partnership

Duffy, B (1998) *Supporting Creativity and Imagination in the Early Years*. Buckingham: Open University Press

Edwards, C P, Pope C, and Springate K W (1995) The Lion Comes Out of the Stone: Helping Young Children Achieve Their Creative Potential. *Dimensions of Early Childhood* 23 (4, Fall)

Harland J, Lord P, Stott A, Kinder K, Lamont E and Ashworth M (2005) *The arts-education interface: a mutual learning triangle?* National Foundation for Educational Research

Oagliari P, Guidici C, Project Zero and Reggio Children (2001) *Making Learning Visible, Children as individual and group learners*. Reggio Emilia: Reggio Children

Perkins, S (1998) *Seeing, making, doing – creative development in early years settings*. The British American Arts Association

10

Facilitating creative learning in dance education

Kerry Chappell

Introduction

Around the new millennium, the Laban Education and Community Programme[1] was frequently approached to provide creativity via school and community dance projects. As the programme's projects manager, I began to question creativity as a concept within children's dance; one which was often assumed, but rarely critiqued. Because of the creativity rhetoric in England in the wake of the NACCCE Report (1999), questions arose about the nature and nurture of creativity in dance education, as well as the what and how of creative learning. Ultimately this led to a conceptual and empirical research study focusing on creativity in dance education in the upper end of the primary school.

At the heart of the research was the dance education practice of three teachers in the Laban Programme. They are hybrid professionals, at the same time dance educators and dance artists, who are often employed to teach on short-term projects; they are distinguishable from permanent school-based dance teachers. During the research, two of the specialist dance teachers were teaching in primary school projects; the third was teaching out-of-school dance classes for 8 to 11 year-olds at Laban.

Investigations were grounded within a qualitative interpretive stance, acknowledging reality as being socially constructed (Marshall and Rossman, 1995) and using Stenhouse's (1985) multi-case educational case study approach. Data was collected and reflected upon using stimulated recall semi-structured interviews, participant observation, video and photography, documentation and reflective diaries. Fieldwork, analysis and interpretation were undertaken in a cyclical fashion, analysis informing further data collection (Strauss and Corbin, 1990).

Creative learning – developing definitions

The analysis generated four key elements involved in creative learning within the dance context:

- immersion in being the dance

- an emphasis on physical imagination

- the inter-relationship of generating and honing-in-on original ideas

- an ability to capture ideas using intuition grounded in aesthetic awareness.

For the teachers, aesthetic awareness at this level meant 'what feels ... or looks right and for what reason...on an intellectual level as well as an intuitive or gut reaction' (all quotes taken from section 5.3 Chappell, 2006).

Generic definitions of creative learning were developing alongside this research, one of which resonated with these elements. Spendlove *et al* (2005) stated that 'creative learning develops our capacity for imaginative activity, leading to outcomes which are judged by appropriate observers to be original and of value'. Imagination, appropriateness and originality, then, were common elements. The importance of ideas and outcomes which are captured or selected for their aesthetic value was core to the dance study and also reflected Spendlove *et al*'s definition.

This generic definition provided a frame within which to consider how creative learning is developed in dance. The dance study and the creative learning definition continued to develop in parallel, with the generic definition refined further within the Progression in Creative Learning (PICL) Study (Craft *et al*, 2006). This focused on music and English, and defined creative learning as

> significant imaginative achievement as evidenced in the creation of new knowledge as determined by the imaginative insight of the person or persons responsible and judged by appropriate observers to be both original and of value as situated in different domain contexts. (Craft *et al*, 2006, p 79)

The inclusion of two additional related elements was particularly important in contributing to understanding creative learning in dance education. These elements were the idea of making 'new knowledge' and also the idea of creative learning as being 'situated in different domain [subject, or discipline] contexts'. As the dance study developed, I became involved in the PICL Study, and had also begun research into creative science teaching (Chappell and Craft, 2006). Working on these projects simultaneously, it became increasingly apparent to me that although creative learning in dance, music, English and science all include imagination, appropriateness and originality, how these elements relate to each other is distinct to each domain. This distinctiveness seemed to depend on the kind of knowledge that is valued, and which ways of 'knowing' are accordingly fostered in the classroom.

Within dance education, aesthetic knowledge in tandem with 'embodied knowing' was highly valued. This was grounded in being able to sense movement from within – kinaesthetic or physical awareness – and the ability to 'think physically', which meant that children were able to make meaning physically to interpret and create movement. It also required an understanding of 'whole self-awareness', 'a sense of their own personal physical self ... of the being ... inhabiting your body' (all quotes taken from section 5.1 Chappell, 2006).

Because of their impact on how creative learning was manifest in children's behaviours, it is important to understand the significance of the dance teachers' placing very high value on aesthetic and embodied knowing. Recently, Bannon and Sanderson (2001) argued for a re-evaluation of aesthetic experience in dance pedagogy. They argued that there is a 'political and cultural reluctance in the UK to accept the value, or even the existence, of the knowledge, embodied in dance experience' (p11). They proposed that this embodied knowledge is intrinsic to aesthetic experience which is '...founded in our senses, realised through our living body in its wholeness, actualised in our words, our work, and daily life' (Fraleigh and Hanstein, 1999, p190).

Bannon and Sanderson (2000) draw on Reid's (1969) arguments that art education is a way of intentionally activating aesthetic encounters. This is similar to Reid's argument for the educational acceptance of aesthetic knowledge grounded in embodied, felt understanding, 'with the cognitive and affective indivisibly united and fused' (Reid, 1986 p24,) as a unique form of knowledge. Reid's work in turn draws on Ryle's (1949) distinctions between 'knowing this' alongside 'knowledge that', as propositional knowledge of concepts. Ryle suggests that such propositional knowledge contrasts with 'knowing how' which is procedural knowledge – i.e. knowing how to do something.

The kind of knowledge predominantly valued within this dance study was embodied knowing intrinsic to 'knowing this'. This contrasted with the way in which 'knowing that' was predominantly valued in the parallel science study (Chappell and Craft, 2006). The kind of knowledge which is predominantly valued in any domain leads to different expressions of creative learning.

How did teachers encourage creative learning?

The teachers worked to achieve aesthetic and embodied knowing by encouraging children to intertwine their personal and collective voice with their craft and compositional knowledge. Their voice concerned meaning embodied in children's movement, and how they wanted to communicate it physically. Their craft and compositional knowledge was structured within Laban's framework of body and action, relationships, space and dynamics, and basic solo and collaborative compositional skills. These are found in Gough (1999) and Smith-Autard's (2002) dance teaching models, of which all three teachers were cognizant.

How the teachers encouraged creative learning was rooted in the ongoing dance education debate between expression and form. As Cooper (1999) has argued, this debate is no longer framed as the two alternatives of expressionism (i.e. art as products of feelings publicly expressed and capable of evoking the same feelings in others) versus formalism (i.e. aesthetic experience as the education of perception of formal, structural and relational qualities discernable through sense perception and in symbolic expressions). The discourse in dance teaching now focuses on how the two might be intertwined and balanced.

When facilitating creative learning, the teachers in this study were encouraging the children to intertwine personal/collective voice (which is related to expressionism), and craft/compositional knowledge (which is related to formalism), with the aim of helping children understand the aesthetic conventions of how movement form can creatively communicate their ideas. Thus, children were coming to value 'embodied knowing this' as the guiding principle for capturing their own ideas in dance.

So what did this mean in practice? The teachers were all using strategies from three core pedagogical spectra (see Table 10.1).

Creative Source: Inside out or outside in?

This first spectrum is concerned with whether the creative source for dance ideas was prioritised within the children (thus working 'inside out'), or within

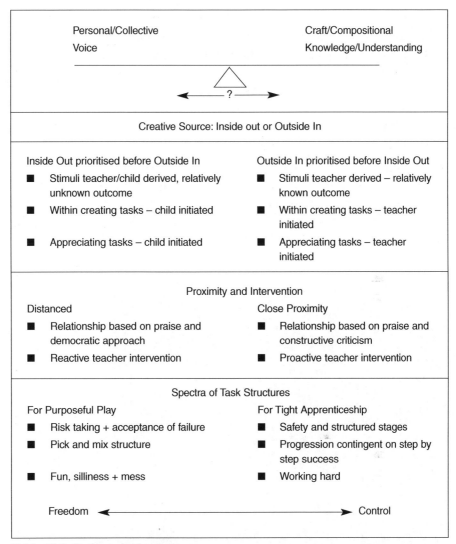

Personal/Collective
Voice

Craft/Compositional
Knowledge/Understanding

?

Creative Source: Inside out or Outside In

Inside Out prioritised before Outside In
■ Stimuli teacher/child derived, relatively unknown outcome
■ Within creating tasks – child initiated
■ Appreciating tasks – child initiated

Outside In prioritised before Inside Out
■ Stimuli teacher derived – relatively known outcome
■ Within creating tasks – teacher initiated
■ Appreciating tasks – teacher initiated

Proximity and Intervention

Distanced
■ Relationship based on praise and democratic approach
■ Reactive teacher intervention

Close Proximity
■ Relationship based on praise and constructive criticism
■ Proactive teacher intervention

Spectra of Task Structures

For Purposeful Play
■ Risk taking + acceptance of failure
■ Pick and mix structure
■ Fun, silliness + mess

For Tight Apprenticeship
■ Safety and structured stages
■ Progression contingent on step by step success
■ Working hard

Freedom ◄————————————————► Control

Table 10.1: Pedagogical spectra

dance knowledge (often manifested within the teacher), and thus working 'outside in'. Pedagogically, prioritising inside out, but including working outside in meant that stimuli were teacher/child derived through discussion, with relatively unknown outcomes, with the onus of movement-generation resting with the children. Prioritising outside in meant that stimuli were initially teacher-derived with relatively pre-envisioned outcomes, and begun with clear teacher-initiated demonstrations.

Working inside out was, however, never submerged by working outside in. These practitioners taught so that by allowing for working inside out via whichever prioritisation of approaches was appropriate, children could authentically and creatively give voice to dance ideas which were aesthetically meaningful to them. At the heart of this was the teachers' ability to facilitate creative learning in dance by responsively sharing and shifting responsibility for the source of creative dance ideas between teacher and learners.

Proximity and intervention

This spectrum ranged from supporting and challenging reactively from a distance or proactively at close range. A praise-based democratic approach accommodating choice and challenge meant supporting reactively from a distance, allowing children to instigate their own journeys (see Figure 10.1). For example, interventions occurred via open questions, suggesting that teacher's ideas might be included, or not.

Figure 10.1: Circulating without intervening

At the other end of the spectrum the teachers supported the children by trying to give security with a more control-based emphasis on craft and compositional knowledge. Challenge came through focused criticism, often proactively using question clusters such as: 'How are you going to do this smooth turn?' 'How do you control it?'.

This spectrum indicates the freedom and space allowed for creativity and the teacher/learner power balance. The reactive end of the spectrum echoes Cremin *et al*'s (2006) observation of invisible pedagogy: teachers positioning themselves 'off centre-stage'. Contrastingly, proactivity resonates with Lavender and Predock-Linnell's (2001) argument within dance for teacher-generated criticality which challenges students and encourages them to engage in critical struggle in relation to their own work and that of their peers.

Within the creative learning literature, the dialogical, reactive end of the spectrum is more commonly foregrounded as a pedagogical strategy for encouraging creative learning, with less emphasis placed on pro-active critical challenges (Cremin *et al*, 2006; Odena, 2003). Perhaps because of the onus in this dance study on unpacking the relationship between knowledge and creative learning within dance, the findings foreground proactive intervention as equally useful alongside reactive and invisible pedagogies. It is thus suggested that pro-active critical interventions may be an overlooked ingredient in discussions of the 'how' of creative learning.

Spectrum of task structures

This spectrum concerns responsibility sharing for creative activities: immediate or gradual. Immediate responsibility shared with children involved 'purposeful play' characterised by 'risk taking' (see Figure 10.2) and 'learning through mistakes...knowing that they can fail and get back up again, and nobody says anything'.

Figure 10.2: Physical risk taking; playing with responses

A pick and mix structure characterised purposeful play; teachers offered choice about parts of stimuli and ideas to develop, including going beyond the task, giving 'as much freedom as possible', with play stimuli and rules negotiated with the teacher relating to craft and compositional knowledge. Communal fun, silliness and mess were fundamental, as was physical imagination rooted within embodied knowing. Tasks were structured so as to balance freedom to explore playfully with experience of craft and compositional knowledge. The key to achieving this balance was nurturing the students' understanding of aesthetic awareness which informed their ability to intertwine freedom and structure.

More gradual responsibility sharing was achieved using tightly parametered apprenticeship. Three learning stages were modelled to provide secure foundations:

> First stage is...where you're looking for physical imagination ... learning skills ... gaining confidence ... a given movement vocabulary ... Second stage ... you introduce a theme, image, context ... asking them to layer ... a dynamic interpretation of material ... third stage is where you're hoping to see the two fusing ... independently using the physical and the dynamic to translate ... the theme ... into their movement. (from section 5.4, Chappell, 2006)

As children progressed and succeeded, more choice and variety was offered. This structure is reminiscent of Kane's (1996) cognitive apprenticeship where dance students are scaffolded through a knowledgeable expert's processes, using modelling, coaching; ultimately seeing the teacher fade from scaffolding learning as the student becomes more autonomous.

At both ends of this spectrum the dance teachers shared responsibility for creative activities with children, but in different ways. As with the other spectra, choice of application depended on weighing a multitude of factors: the teachers' own way; the children's needs; project objectives and agendas; time; the dominant learning culture; the support and expectation of colleagues; and the physical environment. Careful application allowed for varied experiences of the balance between craft and compositional knowledge and personal voice to develop 'knowing this' when facilitating creative learning in this dance education context.

Conclusions and implications

Framed within Craft *et al*'s, (2006) definition of creative learning, these findings show the subtle and complex use of three intertwined pedagogical spectra to facilitate creative learning in primary dance education. The findings emphasise the importance of the use of the terms 'new knowledge' and 'different domain contexts' when discussing the 'what' and 'how' of creative learning.

Within this dance study, new knowledge was embodied and aesthetic. It was closely related to Reid's (1969) articulation of 'knowing this' as a unique knowledge form. When considering how teachers facilitated creative learning, embodied aesthetic knowledge was the glue that held together personal and collective voice and craft and compositional knowledge, balancing expression and form.

This strongly echoes Bannon and Sanderson's (2000) call for a re-evaluation of aesthetic experience within dance education. This, perhaps, has implications in other domains, both those which value the aesthetic such as other art forms, and those that recognise it less actively such as the sciences. Other studies have provided examples from creative writing and music of formulaic approaches dampening learners' originality within creative learning (Craft *et al*, 2006), and there is concern within dance education that formulaic choreography is too common (Jobbins, 2006). It might be suggested that what is missing in these scenarios is the ability of teacher and learner to respond to developing ideas with informed aesthetic understanding. Grasping and unpacking the significance of embodiment, and the connected concepts of 'knowing this' and the aesthetic, within and beyond dance and arts contexts, might prove useful across the curriculum for invigorating learning which currently names itself as creative but somehow falls short.

Understanding and applying different levels of originality is also important within creative learning, particularly what has been called 'individual originality' where originality for a particular child is considered sufficient to count as creative (NACCCE, 1999, p30). These findings demonstrate the importance to the dance teachers of creative learning manifested in valued domain knowledge. If too high a value is placed on individual originality, without adequately acknowledging domain knowledge and values, children who might function beyond individual originality, in whatever domain, may not have the opportunity to thrive. These findings imply that awareness of what the NACCCE Report (1999, p30) calls 'relative originality' (outcomes original relative to peer group) and even 'historic originality' (original in terms of any output in the field) needs to be raised as we further develop our understanding of how to facilitate creative learning in domain-specific and generic contexts.

Thanks are due to Amanda Gough, Kate Johnson, Michael Platt, Sarah Cleary, the children and supporting staff. Thanks particularly to the dance teachers for opening their practice to such close scrutiny. Their questioning spirit vastly enriched the process and outcomes. This research was supported by a Post Graduate Award from the Arts and Humanities Research Council from 2005.

Note

1 Laban is one of the leading London conservatoires for dance artist training. Its Education and Community Programme (www.laban.org/laban/education__community.phtml) provides dance projects, workshops, teacher development and courses nationwide.

References

Bannon, F and Sanderson, P (2000) Experience every moment: Aesthetically significant dance education. *Research in Dance Education*, 1(1), 9-26,

Chappell, K (2006) Creativity within late primary age dance education: Unlocking expert specialist dance teachers' conceptions and approaches. PhD thesis: Laban, London. http://kn.open.ac.uk/public/document.cfm?documentid=8627 (May 2007)

Chappell, K and Craft, A (2006) Creative Science Teaching Labs: New Dimensions in CPD. Paper presented at *British Educational Research Association Annual Conference*, University of Warwick, September 2006

Cooper, D E (Ed) (1999) *A companion to aesthetics.* Oxford: Blackwell

Craft, A, Burnard, P, Grainger, T and Chappell, K (2006) Progression in Creative Learning Study. http://www.creative-partnerships.com/content/researchAndEvaluationProjects/139847/?version=1 (May 2007)

Cremin, T, Craft, A, and Burnard, P (2006) Pedagogy and Possibility Thinking. *International Journal of Thinking Skills and Creativity* 1(2), 108-119

Fraleigh, S H and Hanstein, P (eds) (1999) *Researching Dance Evolving Modes of Enquiry.* Pittsburgh: University of Pittsburgh Press

Gough, M (1999) *Knowing dance: A guide for creative teaching.* London: Dance Books

Jobbins, V (2006) Dance in School – UK. Keynote presentation at dance and the Child international conference, The Hague, 2006

Kane, N J (1996) Teaching dance composition to post secondary students using cognitive apprenticeship and situated cognition. *Impulse* 4(2), 130-141

Lavender, L and Predock-Linnell, J (2001) From improvisation to choreography: The critical bridge. *Research in Dance Education,* 2(2),196-209

Marshall, C and Rossman, G (1995) *Designing qualitative research.* (2nd ed) California: Sage

National Advisory Committee on Creative and Cultural Education (1999) *All our futures: Creative and culture and education.* London: DFEE

Odena, C (2003) Creativity in music education with particular reference to the perceptions of teachers in english secondary schools. Unpublished doctoral thesis, London: Institute of Education

Reid, L. A. (1969) *Meaning in the arts.* London: Allen & Unwin.

Reid, L A (1986) Ways of understanding and education. London: Heinemann Educational Books

Ryle, G (1949) *The concept of mind.* London: Hutchinson

Smith-Autard, J (2002) *The art of dance in education* (2nd ed) London: A and C Black

Spendlove, D, Wyse, D, Craft, A. and Hallgarten, J. (2005) Creative Learning. Unpublished working document, May 2005

Stenhouse, L (1985) Case study methods. In J P Keeves (ed), *Educational Research, Methodology and Measurement: an International Handbook.* Oxford: Pergamon

Strauss, A and Corbin, J (1990) *Basics of qualitative research. Grounded theory procedures and techniques.* London: Sage

11

Promoting children's creativity through teaching and learning in Hong Kong

Veronica Wong Wai-yum

Introduction

Since the launch of educational reform in 2000, educators in Hong Kong have been emphasising that creativity should be one of the generic skills all children should acquire. This chapter discusses a qualitative research study which set out to document the underpinning theoretical foundations for teachers and leaders in promoting young children's creativity. Using interviews, questionnaires and an in-depth case study across three kindergartens, varied perspectives on creativity which were held by the early childhood educational leaders and teachers in Hong Kong were revealed. Issues and challenges in fostering young children's creativity were verified and analysed. It was found that transformational leadership was of vital importance in promoting children's creativity, through conceptualising an approach to creativity, and thus to creative teaching and learning. Reasons are given for why existing approaches are inimical to the development of children's creativity in terms of local culture and learning environments.

Issues and challenges in promoting children's creativity

Several local studies (Chan, 2002; Mellor, 2002; Tsang, 2002; Wong, 2003; Wong *et al*, 2003) reveal the dilemma encountered by the teachers and the issues currently affecting children's creativity. They show that early childhood educators and practitioners are dissatisfied with the situation around children's creativity, despite it being a priority for leaders in Hong Kong. Factors documented in these studies were:

■ *The influence of Chinese culture* – Chinese teachers focus mostly on children's learning to do things the right way and achieving academic skills which emphasises conformity (Mellor, 2002). In Hong Kong, because of the deeply rooted Chinese culture, most of the curriculum emphasises reading, writing and counting, even for children as young as three.

■ *Adult-centred teaching and learning* – In most of the early childhood settings, practitioners emphasise teaching rather than learning (Wong, 2003). In the process of learning, teachers are focused on pre-designed schedules of work, and children are pushed to accomplish the activities. Teaching is mostly teacher-directed and the adult standard is highly valued. Children's interests and the relevance of learning experiences to children's daily life experiences are ignored.

■ *Insufficient time and space* – Due to prescribed schedules, time is so tight that it does not allow children to ponder and experiment. Children are not provided with enough time for imagination and questioning, children's initiatives, peer interaction and discussion are not reinforced. In addition, space is limited: children cannot find enough space for movement, storage for work, or for display (Wong, 2003).

■ *Teaching is product-oriented* – It is obvious that ensuring an output of uniform products may fulfill the expectations of adults but does not encourage children's freedom of choice or creative ways of expression.

Tsang (2002) pointed out that children's involvement in creative activities stimulates their imagination and gives them a high level of motivation for learning. In Hong Kong, however, this critical finding is overlooked. Research undertaken between 1998 and 2002 suggests that teachers focus more on other basic skills than on creativity. The following presents the views of educational leaders in Hong Kong, drawn from group interviews, questionnaires, and a case study.

Leaders' views on creativity

Interviews with eight early childhood leaders echoed with the previous studies on the existing scenario (Wong *et al*, 2003). The interviewees, including early childhood educators, principals and supervisors of kindergartens and child care centres, expressed the view that creativity was of paramount importance for both teachers and children and presented the problems faced by practitioners in Hong Kong.

They perceived that children are imaginative and smart, but that teachers are not sensitive to children as individuals. They described the learning environment as restricted and not structured to foster children's creativity. They reported that children are seldom allowed to generate new ideas: above all, self-initiated ideas and divergent thinking are not encouraged. They saw that children are not free to explore and usually do not dare to be different by making changes and showing original thinking. The leaders also expressed the view that there are many issues affecting the implementation process for enhancing young children's creativity. In their view the problems of cultivating children's creativity are due to the pressures of a cramped curriculum and teachers' incompetence in providing:

- time and opportunities for children to explore and gain experiences

- suitable materials and space for children to express themselves freely and safely

- good questions for widening children's multi-dimensional thinking

- recognition and encouragement to empower children's creative thinking.

Collado (1999) suggests that creativity only flourishes in an environment that provides respect along with freedom for exploration. A rich experiential curriculum, adequate space for children's projects and materials, sufficient or at least flexible time, and a mature and sensitive adult are essential. Local conditions in Hong Kong were not conducive to this approach. A further investigation by an open-ended, semi-structured questionnaire validated what the leaders reported.

Conceptions and practices in fostering children's creativity

The questionnaire survey, with pre-determined categories, involved thirty-three kindergarten teachers from twenty preschools in different areas of Hong Kong. Among them, twelve teachers had more than ten years' teaching experience, and twenty-one had less. Thirty teachers indicated that they knew nothing or little about creativity. Only three teachers thought that they had good knowledge of creativity (Figure 11.1). Most of them emphasised that for anything to be qualified as an innovation it should be recognised by the general public.

When asked whether they were creative in their working with children, only three teachers were positive. The other thirty said they had never been creative, or only occasionally. However, seventeen teachers thought that

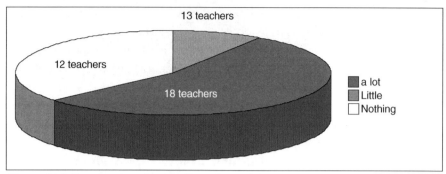

Figure 11.1: Teachers' understanding of creativity

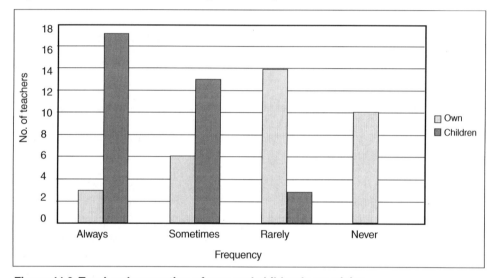

Figure 11.2: Teachers' perception of own and children's creativity

young children are always creative, and thirteen that children sometimes are. Only three teachers thought that young children are rarely creative at school. None would suggest that children are not creative (see Figure 11.2). So it appears that grown-ups are not seen as being as creative as the children. Does this mean that as you grow up, the potential to be creative diminishes, or that creativity is seen by older people as culturally less important or valuable and is therefore socialised out of children through schooling?

As to the relationship between creativity and child development, eighteen teachers responded that child development is related to creativity. These teachers thought that when children grow up, they become more creative. Ten teachers considered the two to be related to some degree, and only four thought there to be no relationship between child development and creativity (Figure 11.3).

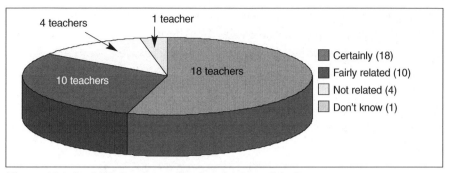

Figure 11.3: Is child development related to creativity?

Creativity was thus considered to be inborn and related to the process of growing up. Nonetheless, all the teachers believed that enhancing children's creativity was significant. Eighteen of them cited it as very important and no one thought it was insignificant. Their reasons were that it improves children's thinking, learning ability and self-confidence. It helps children to solve problems independently and promotes their imagination and communication skills.

Thirty teachers thought that creativity can be enhanced by art, music and movement activities. This explains why teachers considered creativity to be important and yet it is a neglected area: in practice, the school curriculum, influenced by Chinese culture, concentrates mostly on academic subjects. Thus, creativity was not identified as a key objective for children's learning, and environmental factors like the lack of staffing, time and proper materials were identified as difficulties encountered in fostering children's creativity (Figure 11.4).

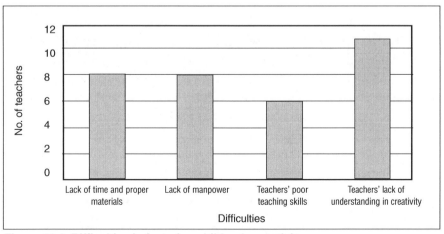

Figure 11.4: Difficulties in fostering children's creativity

Fundamentally, teachers expressed a great need to learn about theoretical foundations and pedagogical strategies for fostering children's creativity: they needed more professional development and more reference books to empower them. This is recommended by the NACCCE Report (1999), which states that to teach creatively, teachers should use imaginative approaches to make learning more interesting, exciting and effective. To promote creative learning, it is vital to have more space and time for children to explore (Figure 11.5).

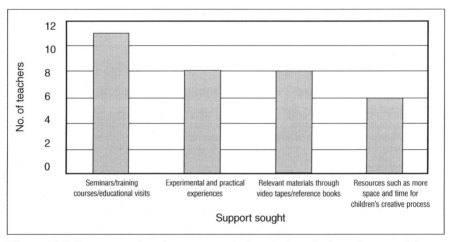

Figure 11.5: Support and assistance sought by teachers in fostering creativity

Changes in perceptions and strategies

The in-depth case study of three principals and 45 teachers from three kindergartens provided meaningful narrative accounts of the changes in the understanding of creativity that have taken place. The 48 subjects participated in professional workshops on creativity and worked on follow-up projects with children. Participant observation was undertaken and interviews, both individual and focus group, arranged. They reported that the workshops were vital in enhancing their understanding of creativity. In the classrooms they were able to observe how children explored and experimented to solve problems in creative ways. Teachers became increasingly sensitive to children's innovative ideas. Evidence of the children's creative thinking and holistic learning astounded some of the teachers. Children's critical thinking alerted the teachers to reflect on their own perceptions.

Through listening and observing, they were able to reinforce the children's discourse and work. They realised that providing children with freedom and time to imagine, discover things and discuss them among peers is more stimulating for children than the instructional model. With experience, their attitudes and pedagogical strategies towards fostering children's creativity were transformed. They said that from the children's work they could promote and witness their originality, fluency, flexibility and elaboration skills.

They agreed that all young children are creative, though their levels of creativity vary (Prentice, 2000). They reflected Craft's argument that creativity should be nurtured and developed through the teaching and learning process and also shared Fryer's ideas that teachers should assess and make use of these opportunities to foster children's creativity (Craft, 2002; Fryer, 1996).

Meanwhile, the three principals also reflected that sharing promotes communication. They confirmed that to be successful leaders, professional development is significant for promoting staff's capacity to learn and manage change. They reflected Day's (2003) argument that leaders should be reflective and willing to integrate theories with practice; they should be strategic thinkers and be able to care for and nurture both children and staff. They agreed with Edwards and Springate (1995) that flexible timetabling would avoid the restrictions caused by rigidly scheduled routines. However, in a culture like Hong Kong, they found it difficult to explain to parents that creative processes are capable of reinforcing children's understanding of themselves, their role in society and the roles of others in their lives and that such self-knowledge is vital for children's self-development and social adjustment (Alvino, 2000).

What have these early childhood leaders learned?

How should leaders promote children's active, creative learning? The principals revealed that it is critical to encourage and support their organisations to build on innovative vision and strategies (Rowe, 2004). The success of children's creative learning depends on staff's willingness to take risks and leave things open for their exploration. Unsuccessful experiments are inevitable before finding ones that work. An important competence for a creative leader would be to read and understand the environment. It is significant for an organisational culture which emphasises shared and unspoken understanding in the minds of their members. A positive organisational culture has a direct impact on how creativity and innovation are received.

Collective leadership, identified to be a valuable asset, provides chances for teachers and children to think more creatively and critically. To develop a strong interest in promoting children's creative learning, it is crucial to foster teamwork within one's own organisation. Besides, from the existing collaborative effort, the early childhood leaders in this study learned that setting up networks for generating and sharing ideas among other organisations would promote teachers' professionalism and creativity. As suggested by Sergiovanni, 'in tomorrow's schools, success will depend upon the ability of leaders to harness the capacity of locals and to enhance sense and meaning and build a community of responsibility' (2005 p55).

Conclusion

In Hong Kong, researchers and parents often value little beyond academic knowledge and skills. Children soon learn that the adults place greater value on academic skills, than on being creative (Bruner, 1986; Wright, 1995; Tsang, 2003). This explains why teaching for creativity has seldom been the focus in early childhood education. Since the overall social and cognitive context is not seen to be highly relevant to generating creativity (Csikszentmihalyi, 1998; Sternberg and Lubart, 1996), children's creativity is not fostered. Thus, the challenges and issues for education leaders are about how to transform the early years settings, and on reviewing teachers' roles.

Professional development is significant for both leaders and teachers: the study discussed in this chapter reveals the changes of mind and insights that can be fostered through exploring a conceptualisation of creativity. If it is then reinforced by practice, this should help teachers gradually to grasp, appreciate and construct the right kind of environment, time and space and resources required for children's creative learning.

To help children to develop curiosity, interest, and enthusiasm in solving problems, the current situation of undue time pressure, over-supervision, and restricted choices of approach and working materials must be reviewed and evaluated. To promote children's creative learning, effective leaders are needed to 'build the capacity for improvement through working collaboratively and building professional learning communities within and between schools' (Harris *et al*, 2003, p2).

References

Alvino, F J (2000) *Art improves the quality of life. A look at art in early childhood settings*. ERIC document: ED447936

Bruner, J (1986) *Actual Minds. Possible worlds*. Harvard: Harvard University Press

Chan, D W (2002) Fostering creativity in schools in Hong Kong: Issues and challenges from a systems perspective. *Education Journal*, 30(1) p1 – 14

Collado, F Y (1999) *The role of spontaneous drawing in the development of children in the early childhood settings*. ERIC document: ED438898

Craft, A. (2002) *Creativity and Early Years Education*. London: Continuum

Csikszentmihalyi, M (1998) Society, culture and person: a systems view of creativity. In R J Sternberg (ed) *The Nature of Creativity* p325-39. Cambridge: Cambridge University Press.

Day, C (2003) Successful leadership in the twenty-first century. In A Harris, C Day, D Hopkins, M Hadfield, A Hargreaves and C Chapman (eds) *Effective Leadership for School Improvement* (p157-179) London: RoutledgeFalmer

Edwards, C P and Springate, K W (1995) *Encouraging creativity in early childhood classrooms.* ERIC Digest ED389474

Fryer, M (1996) *Creative Teaching and Learning.* London: Paul Chapman Publishers

Harris, A Day, C, Hopkins, D, Hadfield, M, Hargreaves, A and Chapman, C (eds) (2003) *Effective leadership for school improvement.* London: RoutledgeFalmer

Mellor, E.J. (2002). Encouraging creative thinking in Hong Kong early childhood services. *Hong Kong Journal of Early Childhood* 1(2) p5-9

National Advisory Committee on Creative and Cultural Education (NACCCE) (1999) *All our futures: Creativity, culture and education.* London: Department for Education and Employment

Prentice R (2000) Creativity: a reaffirmation of its place in early childhood education. *The Curriculum Journal,* 11(2) p145 – 158

Rowe, A (2004) *Creative intelligence, leadership, and the challenge of the future.* London: Pearson Education

Sergiovanni, T (2005) *The Principalship: A reflective practice.* (5th ed). Boston: Allyn and Bacon

Sternberg, R J and Lubart, T I (1996) Investing in creativity. *American Psychologist* 51(7) p677-688

Tsang, S K (2003) Reflection and survey on nurturing creativity thinking in young children (in Chinese) *Hong Kong Journal of Early Childhood* 1(2) p10 – 13

Wong, W Y (2003) The dilemma of early childhood teachers required to carry out a curriculum implementation process: Case studies. *Early Child Development and Care* 173(1) p43 – 53

Wong, W Y, Cheung, H P, Cheung, L H and Wong, K M (2003a) *Enhancing children's integrated learning: Art, music and movement* (in Chinese). Hong Kong: Hong Kong Institute of Education

Wright, S (1995) Cultural influences on children's developing artistry: What can China and Australia learn from each other? *Australian Journal of Early Childhood* 20(3) p39-45

12

Using the AKTEV imagination repertoire to support the creative learning of 5-11 year olds

Pamela Smyth

This chapter offers a toolkit of strategies, the *AKTEV Imagination Repertoire*, for supporting and interpreting children's creative learning. It was developed and tested using qualitative research in primary classrooms in England from 2003 to 2005. The research sought to discover if, and how, the imagination provides a resource for creative learning. It was referenced to the definition of creativity as purposeful imaginative activity and the notion of little-c, everyday or democratic creativity (NACCCE, 1999; Craft, 2001).

This professional enquiry was situated within the continuing discourse about government strategies for raising standards and the place of creativity in the curriculum. This context is described briefly, followed by a summary of the research activities and findings relating to the *AKTEV Imagination Repertoire* and its application to creative learning.

The context

Recommendations in *All Our Futures: Creativity, Culture and Education* highlighted the importance of creativity in education (NACCCE, 1999). However, targets, league tables and an emphasis on basic skills exerted a pressure on schools, squeezing subjects into the tight bands of the timetable and jeopardising creativity in both teachers and those whom they taught.

Designed to raise standards, the National Literacy Strategy (DfEE, 1998) included an ambitious framework of literacy learning objectives for each year group and each term, a teaching procedure known as the literacy hour, and accompanying methodologies were introduced. For many teachers, teaching became a matter of content coverage with multiple objectives delivered through decontextualised worksheets (Smith and Hardman, 2000; Frater, 2002; Myhill, 2001; Wray *et al*, 2002).

The research

The research addressed these issues, discovering that literacy improved when children and teachers used their imagination. A purposive sample of seven primary teachers and 179 children aged 5-11 took part in the research.

Creative learning modules were designed for each year group to meet the literacy objectives through imaginative activity, such as drama, drawing and deepened response to texts. A creative learning process that motivates children to associate, generate, innovate and communicate ideas, MAGIC, was developed to plan the modules.

Many studies support teachers' observations that adding a rich multi-sensory component dramatically improves children's literacy (Root-Bernstein and Root-Bernstein, 1999; D'Arcy, 1998; Bearne and Watson, 2000; Kress, 2000 Eisner, 2002). Deliberations on the sensory and emotional nature of creativity evolved into the AKTEV Imagination Repertoire: **a**uditory, **k**inaesthetic, **t**actile, **e**motional and **v**isual elements of creative learning. AKTEV became the weft across the warp threads of the MAGIC creative learning process and purposeful AKTEV imaginative activities were planned into the literacy modules. Holding each of the AKTEV components as a mnemonic on their fingers helped the children to structure their own ideas in reading, writing and talk. Evidence of AKTEV imaginative thinking was found in children's drawings.

Finding evidence of creativity in drawings

The 179 children in the study were asked to draw the scene that they imagined from the statement, 'A cat was rescued from a tree'. The drawing in Figure 12.1 by 7 year-old Daniel shows a tree, four vehicles, a cat and a person.

This drawing can be interpreted for the sensitivity of the pencil lines, for its implicit narrative, as an indicator of psychological health in comparison with the prowess of other 7 year-olds, or for the veracity of its likeness. Some influential developmental stage theories, commonly seen as indicators of intellectual growth and increasing sophistication in visual realism, were used to analyse the drawings (Goodenough, 1926, Read, 1966, Lowenfeld, 1978,

Figure 12.1. Drawing by boy aged 7

Kellogg, 1969). They were sorted into two categories depending on the inclusion of a human figure in the composition. Whilst all the children represented a tree in their drawing and all but six placed a cat in the tree, 35 children did not include a human figure. In each year group, examples were found of human figures depicted in more or less realistic ways, with more or less constituent body parts in line with developmental stage theories.

However, these age-related generalisations were unhelpful when considering the children's creative effort and the effect of pencil on paper. Indeed, evaluating Daniel's drawing according to a developmental stage might lead us to assess this 7 year-old artist's relative immaturity. Arnheim has asserted that images underlie language – 'visual thinking' and that children differentiate form according to the constraints of the medium (Arnheim, 1969). Efland has discussed extensively the equation, 'intent + materials = graphic form' in his multiple repertoire theory (Efland, 2002). In the quest to discover evidence of creative learning, the drawings were analysed as visual narratives.

Six children inferred that the rescue had already happened and their pictures show a saved cat. Their pictures illustrate the literal meaning of the phrase: A cat was [at some time previously] rescued from a tree. Twenty one children drew a cat in need of rescue with people summoning help or preparing the method of rescue. Their pictures show the tension of an anticipated event and the implied meaning is that a cat was [going to be] rescued from a tree. Most of the children caught the drama of the rescue at the very moment it occurred. Their drawings show the cat being rescued, reportage style, and the figures deployed at the scene to make this happen. Their implied narrative meaning is that a cat was [in the process of being] rescued from a tree. The drawings show that the children used their the imaginative intentions plus materials to produce unique visual narratives that represent nuances of meaning.

Golomb (1992, 2002) showed how children invent visual solutions to the problem of representing three dimensional forms in two dimensional pictorial space. She sees drawn figures as actors within a pictorially represented event, shown by the way they are oriented on vertical, horizontal or diagonal axes, their relative proximity to other figures and objects, and how their legs bend, arms reach and hands grasp. The 'human figure present' category was next subdivided into those in which the means of rescue was shown as a ladder or wall (71), those showing an emergency vehicle at the scene (44), those without ladder, wall or vehicle (17), and those showing a superhero without any of these (17). The drawings were reinterpreted to see how children's creativity was revealed in the way that they invented visual solutions to show the apparent action or stillness of human figures, and their relative position to the ladder or wall.

Because children were asked to draw an event, their compositions included a setting such as homes, woods or parks, with objects such as technology, transport or artefacts, and living things such as humans, animals and plants. Bruner suggests that imagery and symbols are integrated in a multifaceted process of thoughts, emotions, and actions as children construct possible worlds in their drawings: they perceive, feel, and think all at once, and act within the constraints of what they 'perfink' (Bruner, 1986).

Returning to Daniel's drawing (Figure 12.1), we can begin to interpret more fully the creative learning from the meanings implied in the work. We see that it is a dramatic representation of an event in which action is being taken to effect the rescue of the cat. Damage to the stricken tree is shown in the textural marks and shading in the trunk. Its imminent topple is suggested by the angle of the fragile branches and in the strong lines used to depict the structure and to indicate the strategically placed props. Four vehicles at the scene include a broadcast unit and rescue vehicles and show activity dedicated to the rescue as the extended ladder almost reaches the unfortunate cat.

Drawings hold multi-modal information that can be shared with others

(Eisner, 2002, Kress, 2000, Anning and Ring, 2004). The iterative process of drawing uses marks and symbols to give graphic voice to narrative intention from the imagery provided by the imagination. Daniel's drawing shows kinaesthetic understanding in the engineering, tactile understanding in the strength of line and shade, emotional understanding in the mood of imminent and past danger, and visual understanding in the form and balance of the whole composition. If we consider Vygotsky's claim that drawing is 'graphic speech', then auditory understanding is apparent too. The drawing provides an insight into Daniel's AKTEV imagination.

Evidence of this sensory and emotional repertoire for creative learning was also discovered in the other 43 drawings that depicted the event with rescue vehicles, humans and cats. To illustrate this, a descriptive summary is given next of an AKTEV interpretation of Isobel's drawing in Figure 12.2.

Isobel's drawing shows the scene where the cat is about to be rescued from the tree. Three female figures wait whilst a fourth climbs the ladder towards the cat. Three people can be seen through the windows of the fire engine.

The drawing shows evidence of auditory, kinaesthetic, emotional and visual aspects of Isobel's imaginative activity – her creative learning:

Auditory Imagination: Three of the four main figures are speaking: 'come cat';

Figure 12.2: Drawing by girl aged 6

'you said you was looking for help'; and 'help'. Implied are the sounds of the truck arriving with a blast of exhaust fumes.

Kinaesthetic Imagination: The rescuer is drawn in part-profile, with arms stretched sideward and hands grasping the ladder. Her body is bent and the legs are arranged on the diagonal axis to show the climb. Faces in the fire truck peer from the window. The cat is alert and standing on a tree branch, tail curling upward. Birds sit on their nests in the crown of the tree.

Tactile imagination: Colouring pressure differentiates the textures of the tree trunk and crown, jagged tertiary branches hold the ladder and zigzag lines are used for the grass. Rays of sunshine and the flower imply the warmth of a sunny day.

Emotional Imagination: Distress is shown by the open-mouth and call for help of the figure on the far right and her neighbour with down turned mouth and tears.

Visual Imagination: A complex narrative is expressed in the composition. The rescuer is drawn mainly on the diagonal axis, adding to the dramatic tension. The tree is positioned centrally on the vertical axis and the ladder is parallel to the trunk.

Further sets of drawings were analysed with colleagues and found to contain similar evidence of the repertoire of auditory, kinaesthetic, tactile, emotional and visual imaginations that children bring to their creative endeavours. Auditory imagination can be seen in the way children are able to imply sounds, voices and silence. Kinaesthetic imagination can be seen in the way they are able to show that something is happening and can imply action through gesture, stance, reach, grasp and hold of their characters. Tactile imagination can be seen in the way they are able to imply surface qualities and temperature. The children's capacity for emotional imagination can be seen in the way that they are able to imply atmosphere, mood, humour, optimism or fear. Visual imagination is apparent in the way they are able to imply what places, objects and living things look like, and to position them.

The AKTEV Imagination Repertoire offers not only an interpretive instrument for analysing children's creative learning in their representations of their ideas, but also a practical approach to planning for creative learning in classrooms. A brief summary of the AKTEV categories shows how they relate to reading and writing, with examples of activities.

The AKTEV imagination repertoire

Reading and writing demand creativity. Writers use imagination to invent stories of possible worlds inhabited by characters with personalities and purpose, to play with language and ideas in poetry, or to present information and opinion in the style, genre and form that best suits their reader. Readers apply their imagination to the words crafted by writers, and respond to the imagery, witness the events and gather information. The research tested how the AKTEV Imagination Repertoire could be used to facilitate creative learning in literacy. This section summarises what readers and writers do with their imaginations, and activities that foster creative learning.

Auditory Imagination: Writers imply speech and sound: intonation, cadence, loudness, rhythm, tone, tempo, register, melody, discord and silence. Readers respond in inner speech, tuning in to the voice of the writer or narrator, the voices of characters, and sounds of place. According to Vygotsky, the development of imagination is linked to children's development of speech and social interaction. Activities fostering children's creative learning through auditory imagination include poems, chants, rhymes, music, discussion, storytelling, drama, role play, and puppets.

Kinaesthetic Imagination: Writers provide information about events in an imagined world where things happen, and imply activity or stillness, tension or calm. Readers respond by inferring how characters might move and by anticipating possible consequences or actions. Activities that foster children's creative learning through kinaesthetic imagination include dance, mime, drama, visits, wonder-walks, maps, sculpture trails, drawings, making things, mobiles, puppets, kites and outdoor play.

Tactile Imagination: Writers depict an imagined three-dimensional world with landscapes, architecture and objects, by implying the surface features of texture, temperature, weight and structure. Readers respond to these tactile qualities by inferring how things might feel to touch, walk on, wear or brush against. Activities fostering children's creative learning through tactile imagination include paper and textile collage, sculpting malleable materials, printmaking, weaving, feltmaking, painting, sorting and classifying collections, gardening, blockplay and construction.

Emotional Imagination: Writers create circumstances in which their characters make choices, confront an issue and form relationships. Readers respond affectively to mood, atmosphere and vulnerabilities in an imagined situation. According to Cremin (1998), empathy is the understanding that arises from imaginative projection into the thoughts, feelings, attitudes and situation of someone other than the self. Activities fostering children's creative learning through emotional imagination include jokes, poetry, correspondence, biography, literature circles, talk teams, serialised novels, character study, role play, philosophy, history, writing partners, play buddies and mentors.

Visual Imagination: Writers imply how things look through the descriptive languages of imagery, metaphor and analogy. Readers build an internal impression in their mind's eye from these details. Pylyshyn has argued that mental images are descriptive, language-like representations in the brain rather than pictures (Pylyshyn, 2003). Activities fostering children's creative learning through visual imagination include responding to images, buildings, landscapes, objects and texts, making art works, curating, designing symbols, calligraphy, photography, descriptive writing, and computer graphics.

Conclusion

This research has shown how the imagination provides a resource that enables creative learning. The mix of AKTEV activities used in the trialling of the MAGIC creative learning process improved the children's responses to reading and gave stimulus and structure to their writing. The children used AKTEV, involving themselves in comprehensive visualisations of characters, places, objects and events. The teachers used AKTEV to interpret creative learning in art works and in writing, and also as a planning tool.

Since working on AKTEV during the period of research, I have used it with children and teachers in classrooms, in all my courses for English and art and to exemplify cross-curricular courses of study. It has provided the framework for a booklet for parents to develop creativity through AKTEV imaginative activity at home and a web-based resource for art and literacy using the school grounds. Drama and discussion protocols for responding to art work and poetry have further developed it.

My recent work in schools has supported the creative writing of children aged 10-11. In the national curriculum tests, children are assessed on their ability to write imaginative texts that engage the reader's interest. Schools adopting the AKTEV Imagination Repertoire achieved increased results in 2006 and in one school, results for writing increased at Level 5 from 11per cent to 83per cent.

Recent national initiatives have strengthened the place of creativity on the education agenda. *Excellence and Enjoyment* (DfES, 2003) introduced a raft of reforms, including the Primary National Strategy (PNS), with the intention that schools be creative in how they teach and run the school (DfES, 2003). In the revised PNS literacy framework (DfES, 2006), creative response to texts and creative shaping of meaning are now recognised alongside multi-modal experiences, multi-media texts and drama. Currently, school inspectors must evaluate the extent to which the curriculum promotes creativity and give credit for imaginative lessons (Ofsted, 2003). *Creativity: find it, promote it*, confirmed that when teachers deliberately plan for creativity, literacy, self-esteem, motivation and achievement improved (QCA, 2003, Craft, 2001). The Roberts Report, *Nurturing Creativity in Young People* built on the recommendations of *All Our Futures* and presented a policy framework for the future of creativity in education (Roberts, 2006).

It is clear that whilst there is still much to do in primary education in England, creative learning will be at the heart of it in the future.

References

Anning, A and Ring, K (2004) *Making Sense of Children's Drawings*. Maidenhead: OUP/McGraw-Hill Education

Arnheim, R (1969) *Visual Thinking*, Los Angeles: University of California Press

Bearne, E. and Watson, V (2000) *Where Texts and Children Meet*. New York: Routledge

Bruner, J (1986) *Actual Minds, Possible Worlds*. Cambridge, MA: Harvard University Press

Craft, A (2001) *An analysis of research and literature on creativity in education*. London: QCA

Cremin, M. (1998) The Imagination and Originality in English and Classroom Drama. *English in Education* 32(2): 4-13

D'Arcy, P (1998) *Making Sense, Shaping Meaning*. Portsmouth NH: Boynton/Cook/Heinemann Educational Books Inc.

DFEE (1998) *The National Literacy Strategy: A Framework of Objectives*. London, DfEE

DFES (2003) *Excellence and Enjoyment*. Nottingham: DfES Publications

Efland, A D (2002) *Art and Cognition*. New York: Teachers College Press

Eisner, E (2002) *The Arts and the Creation of Mind*. Yale University Press

Frater, G (2002) *Bridges for Literacy: A Survey of Emerging Practice at Key Stages 2 and 3*. London: The Basic Skills Agency

Golomb, C. (1992) *The Child's Creation of a Pictorial World*. Los Angeles: University of California Press

Golomb, C. (2002) *Child Art in Context*. Washington: American Psychological Association

Goodenough, F (1926) *Measurement of Intelligence by Drawing*. New York: Harcourt, Brace and World

Kellogg, R (1969) *Analysing Children's Art*. Palo Alto California: National Press Books

Kress, G (2000) Multimodality. In B Cope and M Kalantzis (eds) *Multiliteracies: Literacy learning and the design of social futures*. South Yarra, Victoria: Macmillan

Lowenfeld, V (1978) *Creative and Mental Growth*. New York: MacMillan

Myhill, D (2001) Writing: Crafting and Creating. *English in Education* 35 (3)

National Advisory Committee on Creative and Cultural Education (1999) *All Our Futures: Creativity, Culture and Education.* London: DfEE

Ofsted (2003) *Handbook for Inspecting Nursery and Primary Schools.* London: DfES

Pylyshyn, Z W (2003) *Seeing and visualizing: It's not what you think.* Cambridge, MA: MIT Press Bradford Books

Qualifications and Curriculum Authority (QCA) (2003) *Creativity: Find it, promote It!* London: Qualifications and Curriculum Authority

Read, H (1966) *Education through Art.* New York: Pantheon

Roberts, P (2006) *Nurturing Creativity in Young People. A Report to Government to Inform Future Policy.* London: Department for Culture, Media and Sport

Root-Bernstein, R and Root-Bernstein, M (1999) *Sparks of Genius.* New York, Houghton Mifflin

Smith, F and Hardman F (2000) Evaluating the effectiveness of the National Literacy. *Educational Studies,* 26 (3)

Wray, D, Medwell, J, Poulson, L and Fox, R (2002) *Teaching Literacy Effectively in the Primary School.* London, RoutledgeFalmer

13

Metacognition and creative learning with American 3-8 year-olds

Ben Mardell, Salome Otami, Terri Turner

During her first week in kindergarten Caroline (4.11) was asked by her teacher if she would like to share her painting of a sunflower with her classmates. Caroline's response was swift and affirmative: 'They [the other kindergarten children] can ask questions and give suggestions about what to add.' That this 4 year-old had such a clear understanding of how a group process could support her learning is noteworthy.

Among the QCA's pedagogical strategies for promoting creative learning is to 'enable children to work together' (QCA, 2005). Given the social nature of learning (Vygotsky, 1978), and the importance of collaboration in creative endeavours (John-Steiner, 2000), this is sound advice. Yet working together, real collaboration, does not occur automatically. It is, in part, based on understandings of learning processes or meta cognition. An example of meta-cognition is the awareness that receiving feedback is a way to improve one's work.

Simply interacting in groups can lead to understandings of how groups work (Azmitia, 1988; Huffaker and Calvert, 2003; Watters and Diezmann, 1997), but imagine the possibilities if practitioners intentionally promoted their students' understandings of group learning. Building on the recommendation that children work together, this chapter opens with the argument that metacognition is central to collaboration. Using examples as illustrations, three propositions about fostering young children's metacognition are suggested as the basis for a conversation about how to further efforts to promote children's understanding of group learning.

The importance of metacognition in group learning

Groups are not created equal. While some groups come together quickly, exude a sense of purpose and vitality, and provide a context for both individual and collective learning, others lack flow and do not promote creative learning.

Making Learning Visible: Children as Individual and Group Learners provides a conceptual framework for understanding how groups become learning groups in early childhood settings (Project Zero and Reggio Children, 2001). It documents a number of situations where young children work together in learning groups.

One example, The City of Reggio Emilia, tells of three 5 year-old boys drawing a map of a city. The map, that comes to include interconnected streets, squares with soccer players practicing, train tracks and a railroad station, houses and power lines, would be impressive in its detail even if drawn by much older children. The group process is equally impressive: two of the boys artfully engage in the third who is initially hesitant to participate in the activity. All three boys establish their own objective which is drawing a city that works, and assess their work by tracing with their figures to make sure that all the streets on the map are connected. Their focus and collaboration lasts for over an hour (www.pz.harvard.edu/mlv).

Educators from around the world have heard the story of The City of Reggio Emilia, as well as other examples of children learning together in the Reggio schools. Often they ask if these three boys are somehow different from the young children they are familiar with. Is there some inborn Italian aesthetic at work? Does the Reggiono-Parmisano cheese that is eaten from infancy somehow create more co-operative children?

Clues to the nature of the children from the Reggio schools are found later in the *Making Learning Visible* book when seven 5 and 6 year-olds are interviewed about group learning. It immediately becomes apparent that these children are different in the sophistication of their metacognitive understandings of collaboration and creative learning.

When asked about the decision making processes in groups Anna replies, 'You've got to agree first, and to do that you have to talk and talk until finally you decide'. She adds: ' Because your brain works better. Because your ideas, when you say them out loud, they keep coming together, and when all the ideas come together you get a gigantic idea! You can think better in a group.'

Later in the interview, the children's analysis is strikingly socio-constructivist:

114

Francesco: If I don't have any more ideas about something, someone else does...

Andrea: And that way the one who doesn't have any more ideas gets another one that goes on top...

Luca: And another one on that one, and another one on that one...

Teacher: Ideas go together?

Luca: They go together like when you're building. You hear them come out of our mouths and they go here [in the middle of the table] and they hook up to Francesco's and Nicola's...

Nicola: But ideas don't have any glue.

Andrea: It's like ... something you have inside you.

Francesco: For example, when you're with a group you feel like you don't know some things, because you're not an expert, and someone else helps you and that way you learn stuff, like building walls, and the thing you learned sticks inside and it never comes off because it sticks to the other ideas you've already got.(Project Zero and Reggio Children, 2001, p322-329)

The mystery of how the children in the Reggio schools can engage in such sophisticated processes and create such high quality products is revealed in this interview. The value of promoting metacognitive understandings becomes clear. While there are many factors that influence a group of children's ability to learn with and from one another, the Reggio experience highlights the relevance of metacognition. These 5 and 6 year-olds have advanced understandings of how groups work and how groups help them learn. The result is an unusual commitment to collaboration.

Promoting metacognition at EPCS

The Eliot Pearson Children's School (EPCS) is a laboratory school, a site for research into teaching and learning, at Tufts University near Boston, USA.

As a laboratory school the faculty is committed to reflective, innovative practice. EPCS's five classrooms serve 78 children aged 3 to 8. Students come from a wide variety of cultural, racial and linguistic backgrounds and family structures: 48 per cent of families are from African, Asian and South American backgrounds; 20 per cent receive tuition assistance. As an inclusion model school, EPCS staff work closely with several school districts to serve many students with special rights: 28 per cent of children have identified special needs.

During the 2005-06 school year staff at EPCS undertook a schoolwide research project to investigate how to create learning groups. Research questions included: How can 3 year-olds become powerful members of their classroom community? and 'How can kindergartners engage themselves and others in small group activities? At the end of the year each teaching team, composed of a head teacher and graduate teaching assistants, documented their work, analysing a specific classroom interaction in light of their research question (Mardell et.al, in press). What follows are brief excerpts from the teachers' documentation that help illustrate the forthcoming three propositions about promoting young children's metacognition.

Creating a narrative about collaborative play
Teachers: Yvonne Lui-Constant, Jill Fishman and Maggie Beinke

One morning the teachers in the two-day a week pre-school (twelve young 3 year-olds) noticed a child trying to push a large rock up a slide. Soon he was joined by one and then another classmate. Eventually, the entire class got involved in the effort to move the rock up the slide, sharing strategies that included using shovels and several children pushing at once. The teachers took photos of the effort, and got the children to write a narrative of the event. This was made into a book that they titled *Super Friends Story-Team Work Picture Book*. This co-constructed story, describing how children collaborate, was read repeatedly to the class.

Helping children discuss their art
Teachers: David Robinson, Lindsay Barton and Rachel Gerber

The 4 year-old classroom (eighteen children) created a series of observational paintings of two cut roses. Done over a ten day period, a photograph of the roses, which wilted over time, was paired with two children's depictions of the flowers. Each child had the opportunity to discuss their paintings with their peers and teachers. The teachers felt that the children were able to engage in deep and meaningful conversations in small groups. This claim is illustrated by a conversation between Emily and Joe, facilitated by their teacher David:

> David: Do you have anything to say about each other's painting?
>
> Joe: There are a lot more lines on Emily's painting.
>
> Emily: Joe's painting is all different colours. It doesn't actually look like the rose because he is using his imagination.
>
> Joe: Artists use their imagination.

Emily: Yeah.

Joe: Sometimes they use lots of colours and use their imagination.

Emily: Sometimes using your imagination could make things look prettier.

Pause

David: Do you have anything more to say?

Emily: At my grandpa's house I saw a painting of a person that was not all done and it reminds me of Joe's painting. The painter was a famous painter.

Joe: I like Emily's painting. I like how she used colours.

David: Did you learn anything from talking about each other's paintings?

Joe: Talking would make me colour the rest, and it would make me think more about colours.

Emily: Talking kind of helps me learn like when I tell my brother Jacob things then he learns

Encouraging reflection on a small group session
Teachers: Ben Mardell, Megina Baker and Irma Hodzic

Assigned to a group to design a new construction area in the kindergarten (eighteen 5 and 6 year-olds) with two classmates, Henry worried, 'What if we can't agree about what to do?' Reassured that almost a year's worth of experience had helped the children work together, Henry, Eamonn, and Luis began making proposals, explaining their ideas, and moving the post-its representing furniture on the floor plan of the area. Their conversation was filled with the language of collaboration:

Luis: How about putting the risers here.

Henry: Yeah, yeah, yeah!

Eamonn: I was thinking the risers could be here and the blocks here.

Henry: How about the blocks on the risers?

Eamonn: No, not there.

Luis: What about next to them here?

Eamonn: That's what I was thinking!

Henry: What do you think if we put the Legos here?

Eamonn: Good idea!

After 50 minutes of work, their teacher Ben asked the boys to reflect on the session. He began by reminding Henry of his concern. When Henry said he was pleased about the group's interactions, Ben asked, 'What helped make this group fun, fair and a good place to learn?' The boys named several factors, such as listening to each other and helping each, other that had been mentioned in previous class discussions on this topic. Ben then read a brief segment of his observational notes, which included some of the boys' dialogue. Hearing this, Henry suggested adding 'encouraging others' to a list of ideas generated by the class over the course of the year about what helps groups work well together.

Promoting young children's metacognition

For children to work in groups is a step in the right direction in promoting metacognition (Azmitia, 1988; Huffaker and Calvert, 2003; Watters and Diezmann, 1997). Yet the experiences in Reggio Emilia and EPCS strongly suggest that teachers can do more. We make three propositions – hypotheses that we hope will be debated, modified and tested by further classroom enquiry.

1. Providing opportunities for children to build theories about learning in groups promotes metacognitive understandings

This works well when children have a space to share and reflect on ideas. Young children construct knowledge when teachers make it possible for them to share, reflect and build theories. It is what kindergarten teacher Ben did by asking Henry, Eamonn and Luis what made their small group session 'fair, fun and a good place to learn'. It is what 4 year-old teacher David did when he asked Emily and Joe, 'Did you learn anything from talking about each other's paintings?'

David's role was to open a space for his pupils to discuss their work together. Although his question has appeared closed-ended to some reviewers, it speaks to the spirit and ease of the conversation that his query elicited far more than a simple yes or no from Emily and Joe.

Ben's role mirrors David's in that his question also opened a space for his students to discuss their work together. With these slightly older children, he takes the process a step further, adding Henry's idea about 'encouraging others' to the whole class list about successful group work. This chart represents the kindergartners' collective body of knowledge on the subject, and allowed the group to continue this conversation over the course of the school year, modifying, changing and adding ideas. Children share expertise, debate ideas, and construct collective understandings of how groups work.

2. Stories about group learning help foster metacognition

While children may naturally reflect on their learning, what supports learning in any given situation can be fairly oblique, especially to the participants. For example, children who are engaged in a heated conversation may be unaware of how the ideas of others in the group help their thinking develop. Hearing an interpretation about how the learning has taken place makes learning processes visible. This is what the two-day pre-school teachers did when they created a narrative about their students' play. It is what kindergarten teacher Ben did when he shared his observational notes with Henry, Eamonn and Luis. This structuring of experience by the teacher is consistent with an apprenticeship approach to learning (Rogoff, 1990). In this case, the apprenticeship is in understanding the working of groups.

Such stories need not be confined to personal learning tales. The story of The City of Reggio Emilia can be shared with children to help launch a conversation about what helps people learn in groups. The existence of such group learning stories raises an interesting pedagogical question: is it more effective to use narratives from within or from outside one's context? Our sense is that both approaches have value. The advantage of stories such as The City of Reggio Emilia is that they are impersonal; no one in the group is put in the spotlight in a negative or positive way.

The advantage of stories from within one's context is that they are personal. This makes them compelling. Lessons drawn from these stories are also directly applicable to classroom life. At EPCS we start with a story like The City of Reggio Emilia to give the children practice in undertaking such discussions. We then ask them if they would like to hear this type of learning story about themselves. The answer is always affirmative.

3. Documentation can support conversations that promote metacognition

As tools for further learning, photographs, video, transcripts and examples of work can aid young children's memories, and provide reference points for conversations. The photographs of the pre-school students pushing a rock on the slide helped remind these 3 year-olds of that particular morning. With their paintings in front of them, Emily and Joe could refer directly to their work as they conversed. The usefulness of images in engaging children and adults alike is why the story of The City of Reggio Emilia is told with photographs as well as words.

The power of images is one reason why teachers at EPCS share video of their students working together to launch classroom conversations about group learning. The most fruitful of the kindergartners' discussions about their list of ideas regarding learning groups began by viewing video.

There are also low-tech options. Because it is so easy to use, the 'two pieces of paper' option is employed far more frequently than video at EPCS. As the name suggests, this option involves a teacher showing children two pieces of work such as paintings of two children who worked side by side at the easel, or the drawings of a student before and after they received feedback from the group. Such presentations have a dramatic impact; it is plain to see the positive results of sharing ideas or receiving feedback.

Reggio educator Carlina Rinaldi (2006) calls documentation 'an act of love.' Part of her point is that teachers document what they value, and that this message is not lost on children. By documenting creative group learning, we are sending an important message to our students.

***

It is important to note that the efforts at promoting metacognition at EPCS occurred within classroom cultures where conversations are common, reflection is valued, and the curriculum is engaging and meaningful to children. At EPCS metacognition is not taught as an isolated skill. Children develop their awarenesses of the workings of groups by participating with others in activities like creating a series of paintings about dying flowers or making a plan for the construction area, and then reflecting on these experiences.

It is also worth noting that this progressive approach to education does not rule out explicit instruction. Working as an inclusion model school, EPCS faculty members realise that children's communication abilities differ, and that they need a variety of support to listen and to be heard. For some children, instruction in pragmatic social skills is essential for them to work collaboratively, and thus develop metacognitive understandings of groups.

It's not automatic

Several years ago researchers from the Making Learning Visible team visited a child care centre in the Boston area, and shared the City of Reggio Emilia story with a group of 4 and 5 year-olds. The children were intrigued by the story and many wanted to draw maps of their own. Three boys got a large piece of paper, and began drawing in separate corners of the page, one drawing a house, the second a car and the third a person. The trio worked quietly until suddenly one child began making large circular shapes on the page. Drawing over his classmates work, he quickly covered the paper with scribble-like marks. Frustrated, the other boys walked away, and the project was over.

Collaboration is not automatic. It is dependent on skills, understandings and a commitment on the part of participants to work together. Kindergartner Caroline's embrace of feedback, while gratifying, was not surprising. She had spent the previous year in EPCS's 4 year-old classroom, engaging in conversations with Emily and Joe and others about classmates' artwork, and hearing stories about her group's learning. She had come to understand and value of feedback.

Though not automatic, creating learning groups is not mysterious. By fostering children's metacognitive understandings early childhood teachers set the stage for creative, collaborative learning.

This article is based, in part, on a keynote address at the Congress of Early Childhood Education in Bogotá, Colombia. Our gratitude for the hard work and intellectual support of our colleagues at the Eliot-Pearson Children's School.

References

Azmitia, M (1988) Peer Interaction and Problem Solving: When are two heads better than one? *Florida International University Journal* 59 (1)

Huffaker D A and Calvert S L (2003). *The New Science Of Learning: Active Learning, Metacognition, and Transfer of Knowledge In E-Learning Applications.* Georgetown: Baywood Publishing

John-Steiner, V (2000) *Creative Collaboration.* Oxford: Oxford University Press

Mardell, B, Leekeenan, D, Given, H, Robinson, D, Merino, B, and Lui-Constant, Y (in press). Zooms: An Experiment in Using Documentation to Promote

School-Wide Teacher Research. http://www.journal.naeyc.org/btj (May 2007)

Project Zero and Reggio Children (2001) *Making Learning Visible: Children as Individual and Group Learners.* Reggio Emilia Italy: Reggio Children

Project Zero and Reggio Children (2006) *The City of Reggio Emilia.* http://pz.harvard.edu/mlv (January 2007)

QCA (2005) *Creativity: Find it, Promote it!* http://www.ncaction.org.uk/creativity/ (May 2007)

Rinaldi, C (2006) *In dialogue with Reggio Emilia: Listening, researching and learning.* London: Routledge

Rogoff, B (1990) *Apprenticeship in thinking: Cognitive development in social context.* New York: Oxford University Press

Vygotsky, L (1978) *Mind in Society.* Cambridge MA: Harvard University Press

Watters J J and Diezmann C M (1997) Optimizing Activities to Meet the Needs of Young Children Gifted in Mathematics and Science. In P Rillero, and J Allison (eds), *Creative Childhood Experiences: Projects, Activity Series and Centers for Early Childhood Education* (p.143-170). Columbus, OH: Clearinghouse for Science, Mathematics and Environmental Education

PART THREE
INTRODUCTION
Why understanding creative learning is so important

Teresa Cremin, Pamela Burnard, Anna Craft

I n recent years, despite the tensions and difficulties experienced from working within national contexts imbued with performativity, teachers across the world have sought to foster children's creative learning. Such creative pedagogues have persisted, taken risks and risen to the challenge as earlier chapters in this volume have demonstrated.

Perhaps the determination and desire of these teachers was driven by their commitment to the potential of creativity and a developing understanding of the value of creative learning. In the European CLASP project for example, discussed in Part One of the book, teachers noted positive outcomes such as increased motivation, emotional development, a realisation of abilities and enhanced self-confidence. Professionals, increasingly conscious of the values associated with and developed through creative endeavour, also recognise the contribution that creative learning can make to social inclusion.

So – why is fostering, and documenting, creative learning so important? In a rapidly changing world, in which technological advances and family structures are constantly shifting, the ability to live with complexity and uncertainty and show empathy and creativity are of critical importance. To enable children to think differently about themselves, their lives and the world in which they live, teachers design creative programmes with imagination and innovation at the centre, seeking to support learners as they take risks and develop resilience and resourcefulness, reflectiveness and reciprocity. In different cultural contexts creativity is now widely recognised as an essential life skill and the case for fostering it is made not only with regard to individuals but also in relation to society and the economy.

The contributors to Part Three, working in the UK, the Caribbean, China and the Gulf Corporation Council (GCC) countries, convey their own understandings of the importance of the twin processes of fostering creative learning and documenting it. In the process they develop specific arguments about the significance of these complementary imaginative acts of participation.

Launching this part of the book through a trialogic conversation Barnes, Scoffham and Hope connect creative learning to a sense of well-being and happiness. They suggest that creative learning results in positive emotions and that this in turn enhances an individual's capacity to develop relationships, resilience and inventiveness. Burgess-Macey and Loewenthal profile the advantages which accrued when children engaged as creative learners in an arts based project, considering the transformative potential of creative learning in relation to culture and the self. Innovation is also central for Gabel-Dunk who notes multiple cognitive, affective and social benefits and argues that creative learning plays a significant role in identity formation and developing self assurance. Exploring the way in which culture constrains creative learning within the GCC Al-Horr posits that unless politics and classroom pedagogies address cultural and social inhibitors of creative thinking, then creative learning cannot be fostered, despite government rhetoric or policy documents which endorse it. Conscious of the importance of assessing creativity, Cheng focuses on the potential of consensual assessment and of observers together judging a product or achievement to be creative, acknowledging the inevitable cultural saturation of such judgements.

Whilst all these authors perceive it is crucial to develop young children's creativity and to nurture their creative learning, there remains some slippage between these concepts, underlining the as-yet emergent nature of the term 'creative learning' and the potential value of further international research, dialogue and debate between practitioners, policy makers and researchers. The question of documentation, how it can help us and why that is significant, also demands greater exploration.

14

A conversation about creative teaching and learning

Jonathan Barnes, Gill Hope, Stephen Scoffham

This chapter is presented as a discussion which raises important questions about creative learning and teaching. The idea of a dialogue which involves two people is one that everyone recognises. What we have devised here is a trialogue, or discussion involving three people. The discussion is structured around a number of prompts from an imaginary convenor. We have included supporting references where relevant.

Our expertise lies in a range of curriculum areas within the 3-11 age range, including geography, history, religious education, art, music and design and technology, and spans 30 years. Despite different backgrounds we share values and believe that understanding the relationships between learning and creativity is of central importance

Convenor: *So let's begin. Stephen you started your career studying philosophy but have come to specialise in geography teaching. How should we interpret the term creativity in a modern context?*

Stephen: Creativity is an elusive concept which leaves many people feeling rather uneasy. This is partly because it's a term which has changed its meaning over the years. Although creativity is now associated with originality and imagination, historically it was linked with the idea of creation. Indeed, creativity, creation and creature all share the same linguistic root and are derived from the Latin verb creare, meaning to produce or make. My work with children and geography has led me towards a wider notion of creativity as an essential component of human thought. Bringing ideas together in new combinations is part of all subjects and is commonly expressed in educational literature. Anna Craft (2001), for example, champions 'possibility thinking' which she argues stands at the heart of all creative processes. Documenting examples and definitions of creative learning is essential if we are going to make sense of this area of our lives.

Gill: If we interpret creativity as Stephen suggests then we need to regard it as a skill rather than a talent. This implies that creativity can be taught. In the UK a key government report, *All Our Futures* (NACCCE 1999), declares 'all people are capable of creative achievement in some area of activity' (p28). Creative learning starts with believing in one's own creativity, involves the confidence to try new ideas and develop existing capabilities. It also frequently involves collaborative rather than individual endeavour. This is particularly relevant nowadays when many people work in teams and modern communication means that few jobs are isolated. *All Our Futures* defines creativity as, 'imaginative activity fashioned so as to produce outcomes that are both original and of value' (NACCCE, p29). This definition has informed government thinking since 1999, but has the disadvantage of linking creative activity only to the useful and purposeful. Creative learning may also be a product of casual experimentation and play where sensitivities, strengths and potentials are explored.

Stephen: You only have to watch a young child playing to see creative learning happening. In adult life creativity isn't so easy to identify but it is just as important. Of course a few special people, the Einsteins, Darwins and Marie Curies of this world, have changed the way we think, but on a humble level each of us draws on creative talents in everyday life. Dealing with a challenging situation, making learning relevant, planning a route, mending a relationship or sorting out our finances can all be creative acts.

Convenor: *It sounds as if you are arguing that promoting creativity may be personally and socially important...*

Gill: It may help us include more types of learners too. When I was researching into children using drawing for designing, one child, Zara, always seemed to think outside the box. The children were asked to design a model of a maze to help Theseus escape from the Minotaur. Zara concentrated her efforts on making a ship for him to escape from a crocodile that was in the river she imagined he would have to cross after escaping. She was thinking and learning more creatively than I had allowed for and was always difficult to assess. I know she did poorly in her national tests of attainment because she didn't answer the question, but was that because she was simply thinking more creatively?

Jonathan: It could be that certain educational cultures teach the creativity *out* of children. I think a sense of our creativity may be a key component in personal feelings of well-being. Recent research, including that commissioned by UNICEF (2007) has made us aware of a significant lack of well-being amongst children in many rich countries. Partly in response to this trend, positive psychologists such as Fredrickson (2004), Seligman (2003) and Csikszentmihalyi (1997) have suggested we spend more effort on promoting the sense of well-being. They assert that positive emotional states are necessary for most transferable learning, playfulness, discovery and invention. Some neuro-scientists also claim that the feeling of joy or personal happiness is the optimal condition for the human organism (Damasio, 2003; Le Doux, 2002; Davidson and Saron, 1997). Their argument suggests that when we feel good we operate at our best.

Convenor: *If this is true, then is the sense of well-being something genetically or environmentally fixed or can we construct it?*

Jonathan: Many factors of happiness *are* controllable. My experience suggests that helping children and teachers feel like creative learners in any respect whatever, is likely also to achieve feelings of well-being, even in those predisposed to more downbeat moods.

Stephen: But when engaged in creative learning we don't usually feel particularly happy. We become so absorbed that we shut out the world around us and time seems to change. However, we do get a reward in the end. Feelings of happiness and well-being flood through us when we look back at the task. It follows from this that people aware of creative challenges on a daily basis could maximise their sense of satisfaction in the longer term and become involved in an upward spiral of personal growth and development.

Convenor: *Why should we encourage creative teaching and learning?*

Gill: Creativity and teaching are linked in two quite different ways. We might teach so that children develop creative products and ideas themselves – this is often termed teaching for creativity. Or we can use the creativity and experience within ourselves to make the act of teaching creative. A person may be a creative teacher but not promote creative learning in their children. But I suppose when we refer to creative teachers we mean those who both teach creatively and promote creativity in others.

Stephen: Jonathan and I have been recently involved in research on creative teaching on behalf of the English initiative, Creative Partnerships (CP) (Grainger, Barnes and Scoffham 2006). We studied eight teachers in schools where the quality of creative teaching was acknowledged as outstanding. Our study involved children 4 -14 in a wide range of subject areas. We found that in every situation the teacher displayed what we called a creative state of mind – awareness of their own creativity and a desire to promote it in others.

We developed a model that highlights three inter-related dimensions of creative practice, namely:

- the personal qualities of the teacher
- the pedagogy they adopt
- the ethos of the class and school

We believe that the interplay between these three dimensions is crucial to understanding creative practice (Figure 14.1).

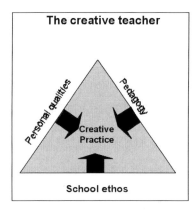

Figure 14.1: Creative practice can be viewed as having a number of different aspects or dimensions

Notice that school ethos provided the foundation upon which other dimensions stood. We also developed a checklist of features which helped us to analyse creative practice (Figure 14.2). These are widely confirmed by the literature.

Jonathan: We suggest that teachers should work to ensure that creative learning happens simply because it makes both teachers and children feel and learn better. Teachers who have discovered their own creativity often wish to share it with others. This may be because as Csikszentmihalyi suggests, 'creativity is a central source of meaning in our lives' and teachers tend to want to share important insights. Creative thinking and learning frequently provokes what he calls a state of flow when we operate at our psychological peak and sense that we are, 'living more fully than during the rest of life' (1997, p1 and 2). Creative learning results in positive emotions. Fredrickson's broaden and build theory (2004) suggests these emotional states result in

Personal qualities	Pedagogy	School ethos
Commitment to children	Using diverse teaching methods	Environment reflects positive values
Desire to learn		
Flexibility and enthusiasm	Identifying entry points for individuals	Environment promotes emotional engagement
Risk taking and curiosity		
Understanding children's needs and interests	Linking ideas	Pupils feel safe, valued and trusted
	Connecting with pupils' lives	
Using humour		Pupils encouraged to speculate and take risks
Secure knowledge base	Using ICT	
	Adopting a questioning stance	Appropriate resources provided
	Encouraging pupils to ask questions	Links with the wider community
	Encouraging independence	Supportive leadership
	Working together	

Figure 14.2: Features of creative teaching (after Grainger, Barnes and Scoffham 2006)

enhanced capacity to build and develop relationships, resilience and inventiveness. Bringing the two theories together suggests a subtle process; perhaps more simply expressed diagrammatically (Figure 14.3):

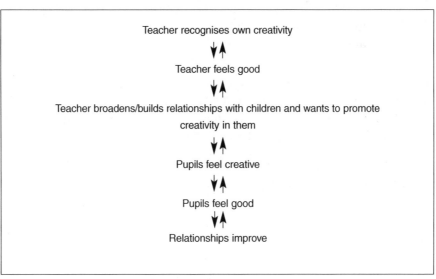

Figure 14.3: Creative practice is enhanced by affirming the teacher's own creativity

Convenor: *Is happiness the only reason to promote creative learning then?*

Stephen: No, creative learning has important economic benefits too. Educationalists have frequently argued that schooling has become divorced from real life. Ken Robinson (2001) argues that we have inherited an education system based on the needs of nineteenth century industry. What he would like to see is one that values creativity, different modes of intelligence and builds links between disciplines in the national as well as personal interest.

There was little room for originality on a production line, but today things have changed. The creative industries account for more than 8 per cent of the UK's gross domestic product and more than 4 per cent of its export income. Human skills are a key resource in many areas of work. From a purely utilitarian point of view it makes sense to nurture and develop creative abilities in young people – 'in the new creative economy it will be people not capital which makes a difference' (Robinson, 2001)

Convenor: *What else needs to be taken into account in education for 3 -11 year olds?*

Stephen: Firstly I suppose that children's attitudes are pretty well set before they leave primary School (McCain and Mustard, 1999) therefore teachers need to be particularly aware of children's attitudes to themselves as learners. Most of us are now familiar with images which show how parts of the brain are activated when we do certain tasks. Learning appears to consist of linking different networks of brain cells together. The evidence from neuro-science has important implications. For instance, neuro-science tells us that we all learn in different ways and that feedback plays a vital part in maintaining and reinforcing neural pathways. Scientists can show that learning involves an emotional component and that we learn better when a subject appears relevant. It's clear that such findings will impact on our understanding of creative learning especially for young people.

Gill: Our current interest in learning and thinking styles is an admission that teachers are conscious that we haven't got it right in education. Despite years of the national curriculum and detailed strategies for literacy and numeracy, there remains in the UK a stubborn tail of underachievement (Sheerman, 2005). Underachievement may result from a number of factors, but I feel involvement in creative activity is part of the solution. Education commentators frequently draw attention to significant percentages of un-motivated and bored children in schools, but exciting, relevant and involving activities can change this. The Creative Partnerships initiative has sought change through creative approaches in schools. Children working in such schools were described as motivated, working harder, acting more responsibly, developing better relationships and more flexible thinkers, (Ofsted, 2006).

Stephen: We also need autonomous learners. What attribute will better serve children facing a future of rapid and uncertain change? Creative approaches to teaching have been shown to develop both independent and transferable learning amongst children. In our research creative teachers show a similar ownership and excitement in their approach to teaching.

Jonathan: Shifting control towards children can have remarkable effects too. In the Higher Education Arts and Schools (HEARTS) project (Barnes and Shirley, 2007), children worked as co-learners with initial teacher education students. When children were given the role of leaders their engagement and creative responses improved dramatically.

Stephen: Geographers too are particularly interested in children's voices. There is now a huge emphasis on the enquiry process in which pupils investigate issues and questions which they themselves decide to investigate. A few years ago Simon Catling (2003) proposed a reworking of the entire curriculum based on children's perceptions and needs. In future a key objective will be to encourage pupils to 'think geographically'. Content no longer dominates. This means teachers will have more scope to promote creative learning.

Gill: Concentrating on design capability in design and technology (D/T) education rather than on specific skills also fosters process skills rather than product orientation. The English national curriculum for D/T for 3 -11 year olds aims to prepare children to participate in tomorrow's rapidly changing technologies and take account of aesthetic, social and environmental issues. It also wants children to become, innovators,' ...autonomous and creative problem-solvers '(DfEE/QCA, 1999,p 90). Taking up Robinson's argument about the utilitarian value of creativity, Daniel Pink (2005) portrays our role in a future 'conceptual age' as needing the capabilities of design, story, symphony, empathy, play and meaning.

Convenor: *So we don't need to be documenting how creativity raises standards?*

Gill: No. That represents a very narrow view of education. Of course standards and basic skills matter, but they alone do not define what it means to be an educated person for the 21st century.

Jonathan: The current emphasis in education has shifted to personalised learning, sustainability and information and communications technology. Each of these foci come as the result of scientific research and will significantly affect the future of education. But the future is much bigger than these things. Today's children may face global warming, environmental degradation, pandemics, and the increased likelihood of global terrorism. Such challenges are not beyond human ingenuity but our education system should be preparing our children for them. To deal with an unpredictable future, tools like creativity, flexibility, resilience, social and emotional intelligence within a system of shared values are the best legacy we can leave our children.

Gill: Sustainability is now a central idea in technology. It is the biggest design challenge that has ever faced the human race: how to procure a high quality of life for all humans without permanently damaging the life and development chances of every other species. Our creative abilities pulled us away from the other primates towards being human as we understand it. Creativity accompanied by self-consciousness and our awareness of complex consequences now underlie our ability to re-invent ourselves.

Stephen: I can't help chipping in here that geography too is centrally concerned with sustainability and quality of places. A sense of belonging and identity is one of its core tenets. Describing the essence or character of a place is a fundamentally spiritual exercise: the Romans had a special phrase for it, the *genius loci*. Aboriginal cultures and ancient religions throughout the world have a long history of respecting and interacting creatively with their environment and the life within it.

Convenor: *So where does this leave us with respect to creative learning? Can you each try to sum up with a key idea.*

Gill: It has been estimated (Joubert, cited in Robinson 2001) that three quarters of the knowledge that will be available in 2050 has not yet been discovered. This suggests that we will need to be increasingly selective when it comes to mastering content.

Stephen: We know that children being educated today can expect to live to the dawn of the 22nd century. They will need to be equipped with high degrees of emotional intelligence, resilience, flexibility and creativity so that they can face any possible future. These attributes happen to be the ones which distinguish us most decisively from automata. It is the precisely those characteristics which make us most human which we need to nurture in the face of an uncertain future.

Jonathan: Creative teaching and learning must be set in a wider context of shared values. It can be put to good or bad purposes. Before embarking upon any creative journey in schools we need first to discuss, agree and document what we believe is good and right and true and beautiful. This is not as difficult as it sounds in a school setting, but ensuring that creativity is used for the good of all is a major challenge for the future of our world.

References

Barnes, J and Shirley, I (2007) Strangely familiar. *Improving Schools,* 10(2): 162-179

Catling, S (2003) Curriculum contested. *Geography* 88 (3) p164- 210

Craft, A, Jeffrey, B and Leibling, M (2001) *Creativity in Education.* London: Continuum

Csikszentmihalyi, M (1997) *Creativity: flow and the psychology of invention.* New York: Harper Perennial

Damasio, A (2003) *Looking for Spinoza; joy sorrow and the feeling brain.* Orlando: Harcourt

Davidson, R and Saron, C (1997) The brain and the emotions. In D. Goleman (ed) *Healing Emotions.* Boston: Shambhala

DfEE/QCA(1999) *The National Curriculum Handbook for Primary Teachers in England.* London: DfEE/QCA

Fredrickson, B (2004) The broaden and build theory of positive emotions. *Philosophical Transactions of the Royal Society London Biological Sciences* 359, p 1367-1377

Grainger, T Barnes, J and Scoffham S (2006) *Creativity Teaching for Tomorrow: fostering a creative state of mind.* Research report, Margate: Creative Partnerships

Le Doux, J (2002) *The Synaptic Self.* New York: Viking

McCain, N and Mustard, J (1999) *Reversing the Real Brain Drain; early years study final report.* Toronto: Canadian Institute for Advanced Research

NACCCE (1999) *All Our Futures: creativity culture and education.* London: DfEE

Ofsted (2006) *Creative Partnerships: initiative and impact.* London: Ofsted

Pink, D (2005) *A Whole New Mind: moving from the information age to the conceptual age.* New York: Riverhead/Penguin

Robinson, K (2001) *Out of Our Minds.* Oxford: Capstone

Seligman, M (2003) *Authentic Happiness.* London: Brearley

Sheerman, B (2005) http://www.barrysheerman.org.uk/record.jsp?type=article&ID=17 (May 2007)

UNICEF (2007) Child Poverty in Perspective: An overview of child well-being in rich countries *Innocenti Report Card 7*, 2007, Florence, UNICEF Innocenti Research Centre 359(1449) p1367-1377

15

Creative learning and calypso: documenting 10 and 11 year-olds' meaning-making

Celia Burgess-Macey and Alex Loewenthal

Why is creative learning important?

To demonstrate why creative learning must be developed in our primary schools, particularly where under-achievement is an issue, we examine children's creative achievements, using our documentation of their learning on the 2003 project Calypso for a Healthy School. The project linked drugs education with calypso music and involved improvisation, drama, movement and masquerade, as well as composing and performing music and lyrics.

Children aged 10 and 11 from three inner-city schools, two in south London (UK) and two in Port of Spain, Trinidad and Tobago (TT), worked with their class teachers and educator and calypsonian Alexander Loewenthal, sometimes known as Alexander D Great. Twenty four groups, of between five and ten pupils wrote, designed and produced their own songs, ultimately performing them at school in special concerts. All workshops and performances were filmed. The majority of the children were of African or African Caribbean heritage. Callender's (1997) research in the UK and Boykin's (1994) in the United States has highlighted the fact that in many schools Black children experience marginalisation of their forms and styles of communication, of their visual, bodily expressive, musical, linguistic and literary cultures. These styles of communication are frequently misunderstood and penalised by mainstream teachers in the UK, who interpret them as unruly and threatening.

Boykin argues that systematic efforts are needed to incorporate Afro cultural ethos into the culture of the classroom in order to liberate the creative learning of Black pupils.

There are many ways for children to be creative learners. Gardner's (1983) theories of multiple intelligences were an important reference point for teachers in both the UK and TT schools. The ability to represent ideas and feelings musically and physically through movement, dance and drama were central to the development of children's thinking and they themselves were aware of this. Teachers in the UK schools expressed frustration that the official discourses of the National Literacy and Numeracy strategies (DfEE 1998 and 1999) allowed for little recognition of children's different learning styles. This was in contrast to teachers in TT where the new primary curriculum made reference to the integrated nature of all learning.

The children's creative learning was analysed by reviewing data from participant observation, video footage, photographs, questionnaires, semi-structured interviews, children's writing, and researchers' reflective notes. The strongest themes which emerged are now examined.

Enjoyment, motivation and multimodal expression

Children expressed their enjoyment of working in new ways, articulating their thinking through multi-modal forms of representation. They used their imagination to express themselves and communicated in many different ways. As Kress (1997) observes, if children operate in more than one mode 'this offers an enormous potential enrichment, cognitively, aesthetically and affectively' (*ibid*, p29). Children also used playful transactions in their co-construction of meaning (Wood and Attfield, 2005). The 'wild energy of children's thinking' described by Egan (Drummond, 1993 p82) was essentially in the imaginative and emotional domain. When children were engaged in creative learning their energy was focused, as in free flow play (Bruce, 1991) and their reflections were insightful. As one child in London put it:

> I thought it was going to be good because we weren't going to be writing it down in our books, why people shouldn't take drugs, and then when we got out of school forgetting it. We were actually going to be putting it in(to) action; because we are always writing things down in our books in PSHE, but for once we weren't going to be writing, we were going to actually tell other people the effect, why they shouldn't take it, and that was better because when it comes to you and you are singing, you know, you think about what you have done and you remember it better.

All groups completed their calypsos, producing lyrics, tunes, musical accompaniment and dramatic stage presentation, including mime and dance, in time for the performance deadline.

Innovating, taking risks, solving problems

For all the children calypso composition was a new challenge. They were encouraged to take risks, engage with difficult and controversial issues, and communicate these ideas to others in non-traditional forms. One group of children (UK) was asked to show the others how far they had progressed in the writing of their song. At first no one volunteered until three boys broke away from the line and proceeded to dance and leap around in an extrovert way, singing and showing off. They stopped and looked embarrassed as if expecting to be reprimanded. Instead Alex complimented them on their energy, showmanship and stage presence which encouraged them to finish the lyric writing in record time.

A group of boys in TT solved the challenge of selecting the best drummer for their performance by literally handing the drum round for each to demonstrate competence, frankly discussing each other's skills and making a democratic decision on who should be chosen. Children in both contexts welcomed the opportunity to take risks, both with the challenging subject matter and their performances.

> In my group we had a rapper and when we performed we were really shy, and we were really scared that people would say horrible stuff about our song...

> When we are doing the rapping it's like he was expressing...

> you're feeling free. He wasn't shy, like seeing if people would say anything. He just got straight to the point and started rapping.

Personal insights and responsibility for learning

The creative context provided opportunities for finding things out about their ability to work together in challenging situations. In one UK group, the pupils sat in a circle whilst a boy with a drumstick alternately played a rhythm on a drum and pointed to other members of the group when he wanted them to sing or play. His role as conductor was not discussed with other members of the group beforehand: it simply occurred and was instantly interpreted and understood by the rest. These skills were based on his playground status, but when questioned, he denied that he was a leader and preferred to defer to the group. Because the end product mattered to the children, they resolved conflicting interests, and managed the time, the different parts of the task and the presentation. A London child said,

At first it was challenging because I didn't work with none of my friends, like the people that I hang around with, and I thought it was kinda hard to teach people .... most of them was just playing around, playing Billy Elliott and it was hard. So I said we have just got to get on... and outside of the project you can do whatever you want, but when we are doing the project you should take it seriously like I do

Collaboration

The process of creating their calypso performances was often collaborative. Children exchanged ideas and meanings with each other, committing themselves emotionally to processes necessary for negotiation. Negotiations took place not only through verbal language but also through finely nuanced and essentially emotional communication involving gesture, gaze, movement and action. They took responsibility for organising themselves and their learning situation, including rehearsing in their own time, and were highly motivated to retain control of the end product.

What was actually going on during the processes of composition and performance was examined in detail. Frequently learners moved backwards and forwards from independent exploration to shared composition. Children were able to make these moves through the same kinds of complex often non-verbal negotiations as in play, whilst retaining control of their eventual performance product. These negotiations included deciding structure and content of the subject matter, taking turns to present and discuss ideas, contributing lyrics, composing the tunes and planning and agreeing the roles to be played in the final performance. From Trinidad and Tobago:

They're doing the dance routine, we're doing the percussion and rhythm and they're doing the singing.

Interviewer. How did you work out who is doing what?

We chose them ourselves.

Children in schools in Trinidad settled almost immediately into their groups. No one argued about where they were allocated. The group work flowed easily with natural leaders emerging who were not challenged by others in the group. In the multicultural UK classrooms the need to resolve tensions between individuals arose more frequently. Sharing involved more difficult negotiations and children were less familiar with group values. Although the calypsos represented the group statement, some UK children were more marginal in its production. Yet the opportunities for sharing in creative learning were welcomed by all children and what they said about this have implications for our work in multicultural and multi-faith schools. For example:

We sat down in groups and talked what we think we should do and eventually we came back with something that we could do and planned it and we worked like that and it seemed to work. We all stuck together and put in our ideas and it was pretty good. Everyone was included and no one was left out. So everyone had something to do and we all listened to each other.

Expression of children's own cultural ideas and values

Creative learning supported the children's cultural identities as well as their identities as learners. It made space in school for children to explore the cultures of home and playground. Teachers showed different degrees of interest in the cultural capital which children brought with them from their homes and communities (Brooker, 2002). In the most productive exchanges they were negotiating both separate and shared identities. Children drew heavily on these 'funds of knowledge' (Moll *et al*, 1992).

Children in both countries were well aware of the threat posed by drugs and crime in their communities. Their shared experience was eloquently expressed in their calypsos. From London:

Don't come round this neighbourhood
'Cause the things you bring ain't no good.
Don't sell your dirty things here
'Cause you'll surely bring a tear to my eye.

They also expressed ideas about the importance of doing the right thing in relation to each other. From Trinidad:

We all do communication to show how equalness is being through our hearts and through our speech ... This is a godly thing that if you want to be part of the Devil's life – I don't think that is the right decision.

And from England:

I liked how we all got together in different groups and all of us worked as a team and helped to make a complete calypso song. First we were all arguing and then my friend she got us all together and put our ideas together. It was hard to write the calypso but we got through it.

How children imagine themselves as performers

Presentation and performance are vital aspects of calypso. Children in the UK schools drew on black musical styles which, though connected to the African diasporic elements of calypso, were more directly modelled on rap and hip hop and performances they had watched on music channels and videos. It was apparent how strongly they identified with these and how skilfully they adapted them in their own group performances. One UK group began their song with a dramatic dance and mime staging of a street fight. Their verses were rapped whilst the chorus line was a repeated chant 'Don't smoke dope, it's your only hope' interspersed with ejaculations like 'Listen to me now'. The group contained a white girl who played the clarinet in the choruses. She stopped playing to rap the third verse, and her kudos in the school rose considerably:

All the crack and all the jack,
Heroin and cocaine,
All the boys in the hood,
Brains are going insane.
Ecstasy and weed,
You do not need.
So don't smoke dope,
It's your only hope.

The children in Trinidad were well versed in calypso stagecraft and style. Performances there are highly crafted and choreographed to reinforce the meaning conveyed in words and music. They were able to create highly professional calypso performances. Some groups worked out complex dance routines involving sweeping arm gestures and expressive mime to illustrate the meaning of the lyrics. There were several songs in the minor key. One group used both the minor key and call and response techniques in the verse of their song, in classic traditional style.

A group of six children in the UK presented a completely choreographed structure. They began with their backs to the audience and turned around in stages to a set percussion routine. The song closed with a mirror image reversal of their opening moves, all designed by the group, much of the work having been done in the playground.

Working with adult creative practitioners in non-formal ways

It was apparent that children benefited from the opportunity to work with a creative teacher who encouraged active engagement, shifted control to the children and offered what Murphy (2004) refers to as personal authenticity, so that they could find relevance and meaning in their activities. For children, particularly in the UK, who are becoming more used to a transmission mode of teaching, the experience of being encouraged and supported in a creative enterprise such as a musical performance, which is seen as high status in popular culture, was liberating.

As an artist practitioner in schools, the calypsonian worked differently from teachers in a number of observable ways. These involved shifting normal boundaries, changing the normal institutional practices of timetabling, classroom organisation and space, and operating outside the dynamics of the expected teacher-pupil discourse.

As a creative adult he was able to take more risks in modelling creative practice for children through guided participation (Rogoff, 1990), and the children appreciated this.

> Alex inspired us a lot, yeah, to start doing the songs, yeah, and he made us more confident, yeah, and like he was singing, doing his calypso songs and us doing our calypso songs, yeah, and if we were stuck or something, yeah, he would come and help us and give us good ideas.

Alex's approach exemplified principles mentioned by Craft and Jeffrey (2004). He kept his focus almost exclusively on the children, encouraged them to believe in their creative identity, identified their creative abilities, made the teaching and learning relevant and encouraged ownership of learning by constantly handing control back to the children. In one observation Alex was sitting on the floor with a group and asked if they had a tune yet. One girl, apparently the leader, said 'no'. However, Alex noticed that another, shyer girl had tried to speak in the affirmative. He leaned in close and asked her to sing her idea to him while he picked it out on the guitar. She began quietly, passing the melody back and forth, and with his encouragement the tune developed and was accepted by the rest of the group.

In Trinidad, Alex was accompanying a group of girls on the guitar. One girl was writing lyrics. Another was reading over her classmate's shoulder. As Alex began to play, the second girl stopped him with a hand gesture, suggesting that his status was not that of a teacher, but as an equal in their endeavours. Formal teacher-student barriers had been broken down.

Implications for developing creative learning in schools

In this chapter we have considered why creative learning is important. In order for it to flourish in schools there need to be more choices open to teachers and children so that they can offer creative learning opportunities through:

- linking curriculum subjects with dimensions like personal, social and emotional learning, health education and citizenship

■ recognising children's multiple intelligences and their ability to use multi-modal communication

■ creating an inclusive learning environment in which children in our multicultural classrooms can draw on their funds of knowledge (Moll *et al*, 1992)

■ encouraging risk taking through working with creative adults, and

■ enabling collaboration and shared responsibility.

Conclusion

The evidence from our research suggests that the processes of creative learning in the calypso project were crucial in stimulating the expression and application of children's own ideas and making it possible for them to bring their own knowledge and understanding into the learning context. Creative teaching and learning enabled children in these inner city areas to access information about the world, with particular reference to their own cultural contexts.

The work acknowledged children's multiple intelligences and different learning styles, particularly their multi-modal meaning making. It allowed them to innovate, take risks and solve problems within the group. Collaborative communication and shared responsibility ensured an inclusive ethos, helping to free children from the constraints of separate subjects and formal pedagogies.

With an increasing focus on the outcomes of education it is particularly important for the human rights of all children that they are equally able to participate in creative learning.

References

Boykin, W (1994) Harvesting talent and culture: African-American children and educational reform. In R Rossi, (ed) *Schools and Students at Risk*. New York: Teachers College Press

Brooker, L (2002) *Starting School-Young Children Learning Cultures*. Buckingham: Open University Press

Bruce, T (1991) *Time to Play in Early Childhood Education*. London: Hodder and Stoughton

Callender, C (1997) *Education for Empowerment – the practice and philosophies of Black teachers*. Stoke-on-Trent: Trentham

Craft, A and Jeffrey, B (2004) Teaching creatively and teaching for creativity: distinctions and relationships. *Educational Studies*, Vol 30 (1) p77-87

DfEE (1998) *The National Literacy Strategy*. London: Department of Education and Employment

DfEE (1999) *The National Numeracy Strategy*. London: Cambridge University Press for DfEE

Drummond, M J.(1993) Assessing Children's Learning. London: David Fulton

Gardner, H (1983) *Frames of Mind: the theory of multiple intelligences.* London: Heinneman

Kress, G. (1997) *Before Writing: rethinking the paths to literacy.* London: Routledge

Moll, L C; Amanti, C, Neff, D and Gonzales, N (1992) Funds of Knowledge for Teaching: Using a Qualitative Approach to Connect Homes and Classrooms. *Theory into Practice,* 31 (2) p132-141

Murphy, P (2004) *Electronics in schools: final evaluation report.* Milton Keynes: Open University

Rogoff, B (1990) *Apprenticeship in Thinking.* New York: Oxford University Press

Wood, E and Attfield, J (2005) *Play, learning and the Early Childhood Curriculum.* London: Paul Chapman

16

Linking learning, creativity and identity-formation with 8 year-olds

Genie Gabel-Dunk

The discussions in this chapter reflect the point of view of a primary practitioner who is involved in ongoing action research. Through four artefacts created by young children – *The Tunnel, The Dragon Car, The Escaping Butterfly House*, and *Ben's Future Car* – in what became known as The Box Project (explained below), developed in an inner London primary school, links between learning, creativity and identity formation are explored. These four artefacts become a focus for scrutinising and discussing the creative learning process: both how the children's creative engagement in an arts-based activity influenced their learning and sense of identity, and why this approach to learning is important to their cognitive and social development.

Setting the stage

The Box Project was developed as an extension to an earlier, small-scale research project supported by the Department for Education and Skills through the Best Practice Research Scholarship scheme. It was envisaged as an activity in which the children could synthesise and give material form to some of the critical and creative thinking skills they had been exploring in earlier stages of the study. They were invited to participate in an experiment with me as fellow researchers. Our working sessions were scheduled to take place after school, one day per week for one and half hours per session over a period of eight weeks. The child researchers were initially provided with 60 large computer packing boxes, an assortment of smaller boxes, large sheets of paper for planning and a variety of pens and pencils for recording ideas. The aim of the activity was to generate a product using more than one box, that the product had to move, and an element of sound had to be connected to the end product. At the children's suggestion, a source of light was added to this list of requirements as the project developed.

Throughout the eight weeks in which the children were involved in working on their Box Project constructions they were offered opportunities to experiment, time to immerse themselves in their learning processes and the encouragement to extend and develop their ideas. Not only were they building tangible manifestations of their ideas, they were developing and reshaping their concept of what was possible within the framework of the activity. They were manipulating, framing and reframing their own identities, with heightened awareness of, and confidence in, their own strengths and competencies.

At the time of writing, I have been able to observe the development of these children over a period of six years, since they were five years old, first as their class teacher and then as a specialist teacher/ researcher in their school. This type of purposeful, focused, creative activity continues to support them and sets them apart from their peers because of their ability to reflect on their own learning, to evaluate their successes and failures realistically and to plan subsequent activities. This chapter reports on a period of the children's work when they were eight years old, three years into working with me.

Pedagogic beliefs and structures

The pedagogical tasks I assumed as a teacher/researcher within the structure of The Box Project embody a concept of teaching and learning that represents the acquisition of knowledge and skills as a developmental and transformational process, together with the formation of personal identity through the medium of an arts-based structure (Cropley, 2001). Examining the belief systems and structures on which The Box Project was predicated through the prism of identity-formation; an interactive, reactive pathway. The project enabled children to explore and develop their personal identity through experimenting with varied roles, experienced through the lens of the community as a whole. Identity thus involved participation and reflection, interpretation and editing, all woven together with evolving meaning and exchanges between the individual and the group. It entailed a special interest in the search for meaning, interpretation and self-construction, realised in tangible works of art.

The methods used to document the project included audio and video recordings, interviews with the children, their creative journals and their class teacher's and my own observational notes and research journals. The child researchers were provided with scope to develop as creative, knowledgeable individuals, capable of working flexibly with their peers in a culture founded on exchange and dialogue within the context of The Box Project activity (Bruner, 1996). The video documentation of the project illustrates how the child researchers were expected to operate with strong self-direction and self-reliance.

Relationships between the discovery of personal meaning, creativity, identity formation

The Box Project provided the structure in which learning, creativity and identity formation were seen as a transformational process which was rooted in participatory activity in which the children assumed personal ownership of and responsibility for both the processes and the end products of their creation (Lillard, 2005). They became the authors of their own personal identity formation within the activity built around a series of tasks, which made up the web of The Box Project. This was envisioned to optimise the process of personal identity formation as an integral component of a holistic creative learning process.

The Box Project embraced the concept that there are interdependencies between learning, creativity and identity and that all three flourish under similar conditions – in collaborative, empowering, open, and trusting environments where knowledge is easily shared, transferred and renewed. Learning, creativity and identity formation often follow a non-linear path and are enhanced through the social component of discussion, debate, and interaction with others.

The interpretation that synergy, generated through the integration of learning, creativity and identity formation, has a beneficial impact at both individual and group levels is supported by comments from the researchers themselves.

Benefits to the individual:

- increased sense of being the origin of one's actions

  'I got to make what I wanted. Nobody told me what to do.'

- improved confidence and strengthened the ability to take risks to experiment with new ideas

Figure 16.1: The Tunnel
height: 1.09 m; length: 4.28 m; width: .53 m
researchers: Josephine Agyei, Aize Ugiagbe
apprentice: Muna Haji-Abdi

> '*I changed from working on my own to making a great long tunnel with a partner.*'

■ increased capability and endurance

> '*I learned to be patient.*'

■ reframed thinking

> '*I told Miss Genie that I wanted someone to help me and I wanted Bryson.*'

■ enabled consideration of problems from different perspectives

> '*And we painted the roof blue and white and the white bits got splotches on it.*'

> '*Clouds.*'

> '*Splotches.*'

■ enhanced motivation

> '*Each week I wanted to see what I could add to my Dragon Car.*'

■ increased personal satisfaction, pride and self-esteem

> '*It says 'Ben's Future Car' on both sides and I can fit in it perfectly. . . . In the end it was made and it looks quite good.*'

■ facilitated the ability to gain acceptance

> '*And on Wednesday, I had to show everyone my Dragon Car, how it moved. And everyone was clapping for my Dragon Car.*'

■ improved insight, thought, concentration to augment existing knowledge base and competences

'I learned that things are delicate and sometimes you have to use stuff very carefully.'

Benefits to the group:

- enhanced collective competence and rise in overall performance

  'If I couldn't figure something out, I could get help from another researcher.'

- enabled breakthrough thinking and development of new ideas

  'Everyone in the group helped make my car balance on the wheels.'

- built new knowledge based on previous knowledge
- increased the overall acquisition of new skills and knowledge

  'In the beginning, I didn't know how to use the acrylic paints and I got mixed up. Now I know what to do and I can show other people.'

- Facilitated the sharing of knowledge and generated enlivened and new knowledge
- increased adaptability and flexibility

  'Sometimes I get ideas from other people in the group and sometimes I can give people ideas or help them.'

Learning is equated with personal meaning-making and is thought to take place when new knowledge or understanding is gained. At a basic level, this learning addresses how best to accomplish something, how something works or how a specific set of tasks is performed. At a more advanced level, deep learning results in more profound understanding, and change occurs through inquiry, reflection and internalisation. Learning is seen as a growing competence to participate in socio-culturally structured activities. Within this framework of learning, the core aspect of the process is not so much the transmission of teachable data; but the transformation of that data. This view of learning is predicated on the transformative, proactive involvement of the learner and the teacher as co-participants, and such learning is vital to creativity and identity formation (Lave and Wenger, 1999; Lillard, 2005).

Creativity is a process of generating possibilities. It is thinking of new things and seeing existing things in different ways focusing on an enabling process in which new possibilities can emerge in the form of ideas, actions and products (Craft *et al*, 1997). It provides opportunities for the participants to experience fluency of thought, flexibility, originality, divergence, discovery of and solutions to problems, risk taking, uncertainty, redefinition and elaboration.

Identity formation is seen as a fluid, ongoing process, much like the concepts of meaning making and creativity. Identity can be selected or developed at the discretion of the individual. Csikszentmihalyi presents identity or self-hood as 'a figment of the imagination, something we create to account for the multiplicity of impressions, emotions, thoughts and feelings that the brain records in consciousness' (Csikszentmihalyi, 1993, p216).

Identity formation can be enhanced through involvement in the creative process by providing the individual with a format in which to direct themselves in focused, purposeful engagement. This stimulates reflexive consciousness and the process provides motivation and reward. The function of motivation in personal development is to energise and direct behaviour towards the creation of a new concept of self-hood, which is consistent with an ongoing sense of identity, initiated when the older order of self is challenged in some way (Csikszentmihalyi, 1993). This type of disturbance to the established, pre-existing concepts finds a parallel in the creative impetus to generate new ideas, actions and/or products.

The process of modification of an older order, the accommodation of un-expected developments or working through an experience of incompleteness has the potential to lead to a new order of being in identity formation and in the arena of creative activity, the pursuit of new concepts, actions and end products (Lillard, 2005; Project Zero/Reggio Children, 2001). The processes the child researchers pursued during The Box Project study exemplify this identity formation process, embedded within a series of creative learning

Figure 16.2:
Ben's Future Car

height: 1 m; length: 1.5 m; width: 1.70 m

researcher: Benjamin Nouroozpour

activities, which resulted in the transformation of a collection of computer containers and random materials, which the children infused with personal meaning in the generation of new ideas and deliberate actions in the production of a concrete end product:

> It took quite a bit of time and thinking to build Ben's Future Car. Sometimes things didn't work properly and I had to do them in a different way. Doing The Box Project, I've learnt that when you are a critical and creative thinker you can invent things from your own brain and make something that nobody thought of before. (Benjamin Nouroozpour, 2004).

A sense of identity gives direction and a personal sense of becoming, of participating in a project which is not yet completed. Accepting this idea of developing identity opens up the opportunity to learn constructively from experiences which do not fit comfortably with previous or present ideas. To use experience as a tool for growth, the individual requires the time and effort to reconstruct and integrate the new with the old and establish a stable continuum in the formation of personal identity. A comparison can be made between this depiction of identity and the application required to bring creative ideas to fruition (Cropley, 2001).

Figure 16.3:
Escaping Butterfly House

height: 1.79 m; length: 2 m; width: 1.04 m

researchers: Hai Piao Hoang, Humera Syed

The child researchers were encouraged to be constantly vigilant in their search for meaning rather than being complacent and overly reliant on habitual behaviours in the organisation of choices for themselves. They were like wandering nomads, moving from the present to the future, meandering through reality, fantasy and the cracks in between, in their efforts to experiment with and generate new ideas and explore other alternatives as they sought to establish and integrate personal concepts of learning, creativity and identity.

> We wanted the butterflies to fly out of the house. We didn't know what to do. We thought and thought and then we used some wire and we attached paper butterflies to the wire and we stuck one end on the door and the other end on part of the wall on the inside of the house. And when we opened the door, all of the butterflies exploded out of the house. (Humera Syed, 2004).

Lave and Wenger describe how learning can be conceptualised as a shift in social position from 'legitimate peripheral participation to more complete membership in a community of practice' (Lave and Wenger, 1999, p83). This theory of learning is grounded in the recognition that learning is both a cognitive and collaborative process. Learners are engaged in a process of acquiring new knowledge as well as changing their modes of participation within a social interactive context. Individuals learn in a group setting through participating in communities of practice. Lave and Wenger (1999) argue that such learning can be shown to have an impact on the establishment of personal and group identities. In this study, identity is conceived of as in flux within the social learning construct of the community.

The detailed documentation of The Box Project study offers a catalogue of events in which the child researchers demonstrate the evolution of their individual sense of self and an identity through the development of their products. This occurred within a community of creative practice and learning in which dialogue was a basic tool in achieving shared meaning (Project Zero/Reggio Children, 2001). Although each of the child researchers possessed a distinct and individualistic persona, they all benefited from and valued their interaction and exchanges as members of the project group. In reviewing the materials, there are many occasions when the dynamics of the group process operates as a facilitator of individual competences and discoveries. '*I used my own boxes and then Josephine used her own, then we put them together. Then we made a tunnel*' (Aize Ugiagbe, 2004).

Conclusion: creative curriculum in the context of The Box Project
In considering the data generated by this project, I have tried to establish trends and significant events, to provide benchmarks for further investigation and development and to highlight why creative learning is important. This study sheds light on the processes and procedures the child researchers chose as tools for developing their inner worlds and the world around them, and their choices of ways to acquire and assimilate knowledge and establish their identity.

The work which emerged from The Box Project research study shows clearly that creative learning plays a significant role in facilitating identity formation and is instrumental in the development of self-assured individuals with unique competences.

References
Bruner, J (1996) *The Culture of Education. Cambridge*, Massachusetts: Harvard University Press

Craft, A with Dugal, J, Dyer, G, Jeffrey, B and Lyons, T (1997) *Can You Teach Creativity?* Nottingham: Education Now Publishing Co-operative

Cropley, A J (2001) *Creativity in Education and Learning: a guide for teachers and educators.* London: Kogan Page

Csikszentmihalyi, M (1993) *The Evolving Self: A psychology for the third millennium.* New York: HarperCollins Publishers Inc

Lave, J and Wenger, E (1999) Legitimate Peripheral Participation. In P Murphy (ed) (1999) *Learners, Learning and Assessment.* London: Paul Chapman Publishing Ltd

Lillard, S (2005) *Montessori: The science behind the genius.* New York: Oxford University Press Inc

Project Zero/Reggio Children (2001) *Making Learning Visible: children as individual and group learners.* Reggio Emilia, Italy: Reggio Children

17

Creative learning
in the Gulf Corporation Council countries

Abdul Aziz Al-Horr

Educational reform is widespread in the Gulf Corporation Council (GCC) countries, a political body comprising Qatar, Saudi Arabia, Oman, United Arab Emirates, Kuwait, and Bahrain. These countries want to establish themselves as knowledge-based societies and to become competitors in today's world economy. The leaders of these countries talk about the need for schools to support creative learning and prepare students to become creative citizens. A huge amount of human and financial resources are devoted to this endeavour.

However, the outcomes are not measuring up to national expectations. The premise of this chapter is that creative thinking is a culturally practised and acquired skill. Hence, it requires a culture that fosters it appropriately, something beyond the adoption of new textbooks or technologies. This chapter examines the way in which culture influences creativity in the Gulf Corporation Council (GCC) countries.

Creativity and culture

Creativity is generally defined as a useful resource that can be applied in a specific context (Oldham and Cummings, 1996; Amabile, 1996). It involves the generation of ideas, solutions, possibilities and alternatives (Smith, 1998).

Amabile (*ibid*) found that the social environment has a primary influence on creativity. Csikszentmihalyi (1996) suggests that creativity does not happen inside an individual's mind, but in the interaction between the person's thoughts and a cultural context. Clegg and Birch (2002) suggest five ways to encourage and support creativity: culture, techniques, personal development, mental energy, and fun. They argue that it is easy for a culture either to foster creativity or to shut it down.

GCC society

The indigenous societies in the GCC countries have much in common: history, religion, ethnicity, language and traditions. They are made up of interrelated tribes, so that the socio-cultural issues in one GCC society can be generalised to the rest of them.

Melikan (1981) indicates that religion, extended families and traditions are powerful in GCC culture and have an impact on institutions and also on social behaviour. Relationships among members of a GCC society are traditionally constant and binding. This is reflected in the values and habits of the society (Hamed, 1993). Although Islam is seen as a frame of reference for appropriate behaviour, when culture and religion conflict, culture sometimes has greater influence on society than religious teachings.

The GCC Culture and Creativity

Melikan (1981) says that GCC culture does not encourage individuality, creativity or innovation, and it is easy to validate this conclusion. It is important to identify the elements of culture that discourage creativity and to look at four layers of society to see how and why they influence individual development and education. These are societal traditions and values, familial structure, pedagogical practice in schools, and the political system.

Societal traditions and values

GCC societies operate with an honour versus shame code, which shapes how children learn, behave, and express themselves in public. For example, it is shameful for a child to express himself in the presence of grownups, especially on social occasions. The word 'shame' is often used to remind children of accepted behaviours. This code is reinforced through other social codes, such as authority attributed to age.

In cultures where accumulated knowledge of traditions and values are highly appreciated, age becomes an asset. Aged people are the custodians of these traditions and represent the social reservoir of collective wisdom. Hence, questioning the thoughts of elders is perceived as questioning the culture and values themselves. This code is reinforced by the well-used proverbs 'he who is older than you by a day is more knowledgeable by a year,' and 'one who does not have an elder, does not have an answer.' Consequently, it is shameful for a person to argue with their elders or question their choices.

Another code of enculturation is the code of conformity, which insinuates that a person should conform to the crowd in his plans and decisions. Hence, extraordinary decisions and ideas are not really appreciated. This is often reinforced by sayings such as, 'do not be a bird chirping away from the gaggle,' or 'the wolf attacks the sheep that goes astray.' These proverbs are frequently used to discourage individuals from thinking outside the social box and to re-inforce the significance of remaining within the traditional boundary of thinking.

These codes are perpetuated and fostered throughout the socialisation pro-cess by parents, community gatherings, and more significantly, by schools.

Alkaied (2004) examined how lay people in Saudi Arabia rate the creativity level in both adaptors and innovators and how they identify the charac-teristics of creativity. He found that Saudis significantly perceive the creativity of adaptors (who prefer structure, conventional rules, established proce-dures, and the practice of the group to which they belong) as more than inno-vators (who prefer less structure, new approaches, unexpected solutions, and restructure problems and issues). Alkaied (2004) relates this result to different factors, the most important of which is the culture, which is fed by family, education, and workplace.

Familial structure

GCC society at large is patriarchic. The man at the top of the social hierarchy is endowed with absolute authority. He draws the boundaries of autonomy and seldom shares power, except gradually with perhaps another male suc-ceeding him, usually the elder son. This restriction of autonomy stands not only against traditions and customs or core beliefs, but also against personal preferences, thoughts, and emotions; it is perpetuated by the societal tolerance of the patriarchic practices, even if it compromises the well-being of a family member.

It is often difficult in this familial setting to develop or practise critical or analytical thinking skills, which are essential skills for creative learning. After all, critical thinking might jeopardise the authority of the patriarch, who is seen as the guardian of the family and its coherence. Children are reared to listen and comply without question. They grow up with assumptions that people in authority know it all, and they transfer these assumptions across other settings, including schools. Such assumptions do not foster creative learning.

This sense of dominance by authority is often carried over for the rest of people's lives. Children in the GCC societies probably move from the ego-centric stage of thinking to an authority-centric one faster than children who are raised in the more participatory societies found in the west. When in school, students tend to rely on teachers' directions, rather than to think creatively.

Pedagogical practice

The schools system in GCC countries is centralised. Policies, curricula, text-books, examinations, and teaching methods all emanate from the central office and the teachers are required to execute the orders from the office (Al-Hafidh, 1973; Al-Horr, 1996, 2003). The curriculum in the GCC countries is quantity oriented; teaching and learning are artificial, leading to rote memorisation which bores students. Students' participation in the classroom is limited and only occurs when they are asked to answer questions or to read from textbooks. Students are seated in rows in overcrowded rooms, which does not encourage face-to-face interactions or group work (Al-Horr and Ropy, 2005; Massiales and Jarrar, 1983).

Jarwan (1999) says that in spite of educational reforms and initiatives in schools in the Arab world, teachers are still considered:

- the only source of knowledge

- the only authority in the classroom

- the one who asks questions

- the one who gives permission to speak

- the one who judges students

- the one who determines what, how, and when students learn according to the pre-prepared syllabus

Such rigid practice does not encourage and promote creative learning in either teachers or students, and produces students who are compliant in following and carrying out instructions.

Clegg and Birch (2002) say that 'it is often easier to stop people from being creative than to enhance their creativity' (p5). They point out that educational processes are designed to get learners through exams and quizzes. This means that students are required to give the answers the examiners want, not original answers, and that there is usually just one right answer on the answer sheet. This system of engaging students in a win-lose struggle to see who is the best does not prepare them to be lifelong learners or unique individuals who can contribute creatively to society.

Fakhrow (1998) shares the same concerns. He stresses that this controlling and didactic style of teaching and learning must change and that creative learning approaches must be embraced if we are to succeed in today's increasingly knowledge-based economy.

Political practice

The political milieu in the GCC societies draws its structure and authority from the tribal structure. The head of the country is the head of the tribe that is the head of other tribes. GCC society is one gargantuan family. The Shaikh's authority is endowed by the same patriarchic system which gives the family male all the authority to practise his role as the custodian of family interests. Many schools teach children to refer to the Emir or the King in the same way they refer to their fathers – papa Khalid or papa Ali.

Questioning the decisions of the head of the state is seen as jeopardising the national interests by compromising his position. Critical and analytical thinking skills have little place in these societies and schools.

Today, the question of reform, especially in the educational setting, is being widely discussed in the GCC countries. The leaders of these countries talk about the need for a new quality of learners, and about the need for education that encourages creative learning, but the outcomes are still not measuring up to the expectations of the leaders.

Attempts at solutions
At the political level

It is not enough for the political leaders to want educational reforms and better schooling outcomes. They need to give a wider window for critical and analytical thinking to the public. This would encourage schools to loosen the restrictions they have on students' thinking and to adopt pedagogies that encourage creative learning.

Some of these aims have been pursued in the United Arab Emirates, specifically in Dubai. In his recent book, *My Vision* (Al-Maktoum, 2006), Mohamed Bin Rashid Al-Maktoum of Dubai encourages young people to be creative and never fear mistakes. He emphasises that leaders should have a short memory for mistakes and a long memory for creative achievements. He says that if a person makes two mistakes in eight cases, he is a success, but if he makes more mistakes than that, we need to find out why. He calls on people, especially young people, to work, produce and create even if they make mistakes. He believes that leaders should engage in counting the achievements, not the failures, otherwise they will lose the race. He argues that the race we are living is not about economic, technological, or natural resources, but a race of creative ideas that utilise whatever is available and maximise its potential. For him, this is the fundamental principal that made Dubai the city it is today.

Based on this vision, Dubai has adopted a new educational reform, which puts creative learning on the top of the agenda. Likewise, the Qatari leaders have adopted a modernistic vision for national political, social and economic reform, which was followed by introducing a new educational reform to help realise such a vision. At the heart of this reform is the adoption of creative learning pedagogy.

The GCC is in need of leaders who think along these lines. They need leaders like Al-Maktoum in Dubai (2006), who believes that bureaucracy and routine can kill creativity, and that the best way to achieve excellence and creativity is to encourage people to live it in their homes, schools, workplaces, and even in places of entertainment.

At the education system level

Creative learning is not about changing textbooks or adopting new technologies. It is a question of cultural practices in schools and at home. The educational reforms in the GCC countries follow what Clegg and Birch (2002) call the 'expert syndrome,' meaning that they impart ready made solutions along with the experts to solve the problems. These experts – generally foreigners to GCC culture and lacking sociological awareness of it – usually to superimpose these ready made solutions arbitrarily. They are familiar with the solution but not the problem; they bring educational solutions which have been developed in a different context with different problems, and which do not necessarily fit the actual needs of GCC schools. Creative learning requires that pedagogies should address the cultural and social inhibitors of creative thinking. Only then can creative learning models be effectively implemented.

At the familial level

Creative learning requires parents to provide their children with a stimulating environment that has books, materials and games suited to the child's developmental age, abilities and skills (Adas, 1998; Amabile, 1983). However, in the GCC countries, very few families have such resources: even those who have well-stocked bookshelves rarely read to their children.

Al-Hammadi (2006) conducted a study examining how young people in GCC countries spend their leisure time, and reported that visiting libraries was rated the last out of eight priorities. This is hardly conducive to the promotion of creative thinking.

For any change to take place, young people need different education, different parenting and a different culture. Parents are expected to encourage their children to experiment with new innovations and ideas, but in GCC culture, parents encourage their children to do things in the traditional and way, and feel uncomfortable about doing things differently (Adas, 1998; Alkaied, 2004; Amabile, 1983; Rice, 2003). They should share their own experiences and appreciation of creative thinking with their children (Adas, *ibid*; Amabile, *ibid*), but the authoritarian relationship between family members discourages such sharing, interaction and exchange within the family.

Conclusion

Supporting creativity at all levels in the family, school, workplace and government requires new a culture and a new mindset. This can only be achieved by:

- increasing the level of commitment of leaders in GCC countries to creative learning

- developing a conceptual framework for creative learning that is culturally sensitive to the GCC context

- disseminating the model to all stakeholders, including parents, schools, communities, workplaces, media and governments

- using the media to express the need for change and the shared responsibility for introducing creativity at all levels

- developing a strategic plan to encourage creative learning GCC-wide

- revisiting GCC culture and tradition, and emphasising elements that support creativity by individuals and groups, and

- redesigning school curricula and programmes to encourage and promote creative learning.

Creative learning is not well documented in the GCC context because the concept has been newly introduced to the educational system through the discrete reform efforts made some countries and on a limited scale.

The overarching theme of this chapter is that the creative potential of individuals and societies in GCC countries should be released through radical new initiatives at all levels, to ensure that everyone has the freedom to be creative and innovative.

References

Adas, M (1998) *Educating Children for Self-Confidence Building and Abilities Development.* Jordan: Dar Al-Fikr

Al-Hafidh, N (1973) *Qatar education profile.* Beirut: Unesco Regional Office for education in the Arab Countries

Al-Hammadi, A (2006) *Survey Study on Leisure Time for Youth Boys and Girls in GCC States.* Riyadh: The Cooperation Council for Arab States of the Gulf – Secretariat General

Al-Horr, A (2003) *Education, development and renaissance.* Beirut: Allprint

Al-Horr, A (1996) Co-operative learning and the new primary science curriculum in the State of Qatar. Unpublished PhD thesis, University of Durham

Al-Horr, A and Ropy, A (2005) Proposed theoretical framework to create learning system promotes teacher/student partnership in the classroom. *Risalat Al-Khaleej Al-Arabi*, 97 (1) p13-61

Alkaied, A (2004) *Cross cultural Perception of Creativity: A Sample from Saudi Arabia. Master of Science.* State University of New York, USA

Al-Maktoum, M (2006) *My Vision: Challenges in the Race for Excellence.* UAE: Motivate Publications

Amabile, T M (1983) *The Social Psychology of Creativity.* NY: Springer-Verlag

Amabile, T M (1996) *Creativity in context. Update to the social Psychology of Creativity.* Boulder, CO: Westview Press

Clegg, B and Birch, P (2002) *Crash course in creativity,* London: Kogan Page Ltd

Csikszentmihalyi, M (1996) *Creativity – Flow and the Psychology of Discovery and Invention.* New York: Harper Collins Publisher

Fakhrow, A (1998) Developing thinking skills, paper submitted to *The First Arab Scientific Conference for Gifted and Talented Students*, UAE

Hamed, A M (1993) Islamic religion in Qatar during the twentieth century: personal and institutional. Unpublished PhD thesis, University of Manchester

Jarwan, F (1999) *Teaching Thinking: Concepts and Applications.* UAE: Dar AL-ketab Al-Jameai

Massiales, B G and Jarrar, S A (1983) *Education in the Arab World.* New York: Praeger Publishers

Melikan, L (1981) *Jassim: A Study in Psychological Development of a Young Man in Qatar.* London: Longman

Oldham, G and Cummings, A C (1996) Employee creativity: Personal and contextual factors. *Academy of Management Journal*, 39 (3) p607-635

Rice, G (2003) The challenge of creativity and culture: a framework for analysis with application to Arabian Gulf Firms. *International Business Review*, 12, p461-477.

Smith, G F (1998) Idea-generation techniques: A formulary of active ingredients. *Journal of Creative Behavior*, 32 (2) p107-133

18

Consensual assessment in creative learning

Vivian M Y Cheng

How to assess student creativity is an important concern in creative learning, but the picture is complex. For a start, creativity may differ from conventional learning objectives in schools. In addition, studies (Cropley, 1999; Lubart, 1999; Runco, 1996) suggest that definition of creativity varies between arts and science, western and eastern people, young and old people, expert and everyday life domains. It is widely believed that creativity is contextually based and that objective criteria are difficult to define. One assessment method which deals with this special contextually-based characteristic of creativity is the consensual assessment technique, or CAT, suggested by Amabile (1982).

The consensual assessment technique

Amabile (1996) suggests that creativity is contextually based and socially defined. It cannot be defined explicitly, but a product is considered to be creative when appropriate judges agree that it is. Appropriate judges are those who are familiar with the field of activity, and may include those who have generated the creative outcomes. The CAT procedure is first to put the creative products in a random order to be considered by judges who have no prior training. They then rate the level of creativity (and other dimensions) of each product independently, on a scale from 'very uncreative, uncreative, average, creative' to 'very creative'.

Many studies report successful uses of CAT in assessing creativity in products. Several studies in the west and east have applied CAT to assess children's creative products including paintings, collages, and musical compositions. Most of these studies report acceptable or high inter-rater reliabilities (Garaigordobile, 2006; Gerrard, Poteat and Ironsmith, 1996; Hickey, 2001; Hennessey and Amabile, 1999; Lin, 2005; Niu and Sternberg, 2001; Qu and Shi, 2005).

What kinds of products?

In past studies, CAT was mostly applied to assess tangible products, like drawing, collages and writing. According to Amabile's theory (1996) and Hennessey and Amabile's elaboration (1999), any open tasks with many possible solutions that can be clearly presented to the judges can be assessed by CAT. Thus, non-tangible ideas in verbal or written reports, behaviours or performances in authentic assessments, and immediate responses in written tests are all assessable by CAT. Educators may therefore consider applying CAT to a range of children's work.

Applying CAT to school learning demands sensitivity on several counts. Amabile (1996) suggests that the creative tasks involved should not be highly dependent on specific skills or knowledge. If they are it may be difficult to distinguish creativity from these two dimensions, and this would threaten the discriminant validity of CAT. Clearly, learning tasks in subject areas are not always free from skill and knowledge demands, but teachers should equip students with adequate skills and knowledge for the task involved so that it is creativity that is assessed rather than knowledge and skill.

CAT may be successfully extended to non-parallel creative products. Studies by Baer *et al* (2004) and Garaigordobile (2006) suggest that pupils' work on different tasks done in different conditions such as drawings on different themes completed in different lessons can be judged together. The explicit instruction, to be creative can have a positive effect on creative performance: Chen *et al* (2005) found this to be the case for both Chinese and US children.

Whose judgments?

In earlier applications, CAT drew on experts in the field as suitable judges. Policastro and Gardner (1995) commented that expert judgment is greatly enriched by years of training in particular disciplines. Though many studies using expert judges reported good reliability and validity (Amabile, 1996, Baer, Kaufman and Gentile, 2004), findings on primary school children's products were mixed. Garaigordobile (2006), Gerrard, Poteat and Ironsmith (1996), Hennessey and Amabile (1999) reported success in using artists to judge the drawings of primary school children. Lin (2005) reported reliability in using music specialists to assess compositions by year 5 students in Taiwan, China. In contrast, Hickey (2001), in assessing musical compositions of fourth and fifth grade children in USA found that the inter-rater reliability of three composers was only .04, much lower than that of teacher or child judges.

Hennessey and Amabile (1999) argue that it is 'the judges' familiarity with the domain that is important, not ...that they themselves may have produced work rated as highly creative' (p351). Many recent studies report success with non-expert judges, reinforcing the perspective that teachers in schools who know the students better may be better judges. Studies report good inter-rater reliability when using schoolteachers as judges of children's products (Gerrard *et al*, 1996; Hargreaves *et al*, 1996; Hennessey and Amabile, 1999; Hickey, 2001).

Does assessing artefacts made by small children require experienced judges? A growing number of CAT projects use peer assessment: Chen *et al* (2002), Christiaans (2002), Hennessey (1994), Niu and Sternberg (2001) and Wolfradt and Pretz (2001) used university students as peer judges in their studies. Kaufman *et al*, (2005), Hsu *et al*, (2002) and Gagne *et al*, (1993) used secondary school students as peer judges in their studies. Nearly all these studies emphasise that it is possible and worthwhile to use peers as judges. Studies investigating primary children as peer judges are rare, although Hickey (2001) reports studying both seventh grade and second grade pupils in the USA as peer judges which had acceptable inter-rater reliabilities among the young judges.

Peer assessment in primary schools has both strengths and weaknesses. Peers can be appropriate judges, because they are most familiar with the creators. Brown (1996) suggests that peer evaluation within a group might reveal individual creativity and contributions to group projects better than their teachers could. Through peer assessment, students learn to appreciate the creativity of others, as well as how to evaluate and judge it. From a practical point of view, using peer judges makes it easier to get a larger panel size for attaining higher levels of inter-rater reliabilities.

However, peer assessment of creativity can be problematic. We need to consider whether or not children have a clear concept of creativity. Are their conceptions consistent with one other's? Can children reach consensus in making judgments, and display acceptable levels of reliability in assessment? Even if they can reach agreement, the extent to which their views align with those of their teachers may vary. Another concern is that small children may not be able to remember large numbers of works before they make comparisons using the CAT process. Do they have the evaluative ability to decide which ideas are either unusual, appropriate or useful to the task in hand?

Most of these questions are still unanswered. Only the last question has been partially addressed by Charles and Runco (2000-01), who found that third grade children already possessed a certain level of ability to distinguish originality and appropriateness of the ideas in common divergent thinking tests, and that these kinds of abilities increased significantly from third to fifth grade. More studies are needed before any conclusions can be drawn about the potential of peer assessment in primary schools.

What values?

In addition to inter-rater reliability, educators need to consider whether expert, teacher and child judges differ in their judgments of creativity in consensual assessment. The empirical findings in this area are mixed. Some studies (Gerrard *et al*, 1996; Hickey, 2001; Hsu *et al*, 2002) highlighted differences between the judgments of pupils, school teachers and experts in the fields, whereas Kaufman *et al*, (2005) and Christiaans (2002) emphasised the similarities between judgments of experts and peers. Focusing on children's work, Hickey (2001) reported ratings of student judges across two different year levels as highly correlated, but not significantly related to the ratings of expert judges.

Discrepancies among different groups of judges may reflect different views of creativity. It is therefore vital to match the means of assessment to the kind of creativity development being targeted.

Approaches to defining creativity in making judgements

There are at least three different ways of defining creativity: the personal, field and peer comparison approaches.

Baer (1997) argued that creativity can be entirely personal. He defines creativity as 'anything someone does in a way that is original to the creator and that is appropriate to the purpose or goal of the creator' (p4). If we want to encourage this personal kind of creativity, self-assessment, where children compare their present performance with their past efforts, may be most appropriate. This avoids the negative impact on self-esteem which can arise from to peer competition, and encourages children to make breakthroughs in their own thinking, without having to worry about whether their ideas are novel to others. Nobody knows better than the creator how the ideas have been developed, and how to judge whether or not they are original.

Self-assessment may be meaningful in formative assessment. It helps students to reflect on their own achievements and to progress in creative learning. However, self-assessment of creativity has innate bias (Priest, 2006), and is not so practical in summative assessments, in which the results are used for selection and screening purposes.

In contrast to Baer's approach, Sternberg and Lubart (1999) suggested that creative products should be novel and appropriate to the people in the field. Creative people are those who regularly produce novel and appropriate ideas in the field. However, primary school children usually lack the advanced domain-specific knowledge and skills required for producing and judging useful ideas in the field and most are unfamiliar with the adult field and do not have the information to distinguish between common and novel ideas. The ability to generate novel and useful products in the field is a strong challenge to young children of average ability. Fryer (1996) and Craft (2002) both pointed out that much less stringent assessment procedures and criteria are appropriate for small children's work. To avoid negative impact on the self-esteem of the young pupils, educators should consider assessing their products in a different way.

Neither the personal nor the field comparison approaches are appropriate for creativity assessments in school education. The third approach defines creativity through peer comparison. CAT is close to this approach, as it requests all judges to review all products and judge one product in comparison with the others. According to Amabile's theory (1996), the judges should be familiar with both the creators and the creative processes. Teachers and children with enough peer understanding are suitable judges if this approach is used.

Locus of judgement

As well as in the locus of comparison, groups of judges may also differ in other aspects when assessing creativity. When judging products, do teachers and children value different things? Do adults value appropriateness and usefulness of ideas more, whereas children appreciate novelty and being funny more? Would pupils consider colourful artworks or skilful writings creative? Can children distinguish aesthetic appeal or technical merit from creativity? These are all unanswered questions.

A study by Cheng (2002) reported that, when some mischievous 9 and 10 year-olds in a primary school classroom suggested increasing the birth rate by enforcing women to bear children by law, and to reduce the problems of an aging population by killing old people, other children supported the proposals, arguing that these were the most 'effective' methods! This may not be a common response, but being ethical is a criterion which children should learn to include in their evaluation of creative ideas (Craft *et al*, in press). And perhaps the locus of assessment should involve both child and teacher dimensions, balancing teacher and pupil roles (Craft, 2002).

Exploring the potential of consensual assessment

The consensual method is a flexible and widely applicable assessment method of creativity. As suitable judges only need to make judgments according to their own implicit theories of creativity in their own context, CAT is adaptable to different subject areas, schools, cultures and age groups. Going beyond the basic differentiating function, consensual assessment method has made several additional contributions to creative learning. Teachers and children read, appreciate and evaluate a great number of creative products: this valuable experience may develop their own interest in creativity pursuits. And consensual assessment can provide important feedback on the learning process. Through self and peer assessments, children learn how to regulate their own creative learning process.

Even though young children may lack mature and consistent conceptions of creativity, peer and self-assessments should not be abandoned in primary schools. Instead, through engagement in making creativity judgments, and negotiating with teachers and pupils when discrepancies arise, both children and teachers can reflect on the meaning of being creative. Involvement in consensual assessment will strengthen the conceptions of creativity of both children and teachers.

Consensual assessment may also encourage children to think more about their own learning. Assessment methods building social consensus could provide more than top-down or standardised assessment criteria, allowing room for pupils to consider what they wish to learn and how. This kind of assessment method tends to give them a stronger feeling of possession of their own learning. As creative learning emphasises the self-direction of children in learning (Jeffrey and Craft, 2004), ability and motivation in thinking about learning are important. Educators may consider the consensual assessment process to be significant part of learning.

With the consensual assessment element included, the purpose of creative learning goes beyond the development of children's creativity. In this educational process children learn to think about their own learning objectives and how these can be achieved and evaluated. Ultimately, they understand how to be creative learners, through creative learning and consensual assessment.

References

Amabile, T M (1982) Social psychology of creativity: A consensual assessment technique. *Journal of Personality and Social Psychology*, 43, p997-1013

Amabile, T (1996) *Creativity in Context.* Colorado: Westview Press

Baer, J (1997) *Creative teachers, creative students.* Needham Heights: Allyn and Bacon

Baer, J, Kaufman, J and Gentile, C (2004) Extension of the consensual assessment technique to nonparallel creative products. *Creativity Research Journal,* 16(1) p113-117

Brown, S (1996) Assessing individual performance on group projects. *Focus on Learning Problems in Mathematics* 18(4) p1-7

Charles, R and Runco, M (2000-2001) Developmental trends in the evaluative and divergent thinking of children. *Creativity Research Journal,* 13(3 and 4) p417-437

Chen, C, Kasof, J, Himsel, A J, Greenberger, E, Dong, Q and Xue, G (2002) Creativity in drawings of geometric shapes. *Journal of Cross-cultural Psychology* 33(2) p171-187

Chen, C, Kasof, J, Himsel, A, Dmitrieva, J, Dong, Q and Xue, G (2005) Effects of explicit instruction to 'be creative' across domains and cultures. *Journal of Creative Behavior* 39(2) p89-110

Cheng, M Y V (2002) Assessing creativity in subject-based written tests (in Chinese). In M Y V Cheng (ed) *Nurturing Creativity – Teaching Practice and School-based Reform.* Hong Kong: University Grant Committee

Christiaans, H (2002) Creativity as a design criterion. *Creativity Research Journal* 14(1) p 41-54

Craft, A (2002) *Creativity and early years education.* London: Continuum

Craft, A, Gardner, H and Claxton, G (in press) *Creativity, Wisdom and Trusteeship: exploring the role of education.* Thousand Oaks CA: Corwin Press

Cropley, A (1999) Definitions of creativity. In M. Runco (ed) *Encyclopedia of Creativity Volume 1.* San Diego: Academic Press p511-524

Fryer, M (1996) *Creative teaching and learning.* London: Paul Chapman

Gagne, F, Begin, J and Talbot, L (1993) How well do peers agree among themselves when nominating the gifted or talented? *Gifted Child Quarterly* 37(1) p39-45

Garaigordobile, M (2006) Intervention in creativity with children aged 10 and 11 years: impact of a play program on verbal and graphic-figural creativity. *Creativity Research Journal* 18(3) p329-345

Gerrard, L, Poteat, G M and Ironsmith, M (1996) Promoting children's creativity: effects of competition, self-esteem, and immunization. *Creativity Research Journal* 9(4) p339-346

Hargreaves, D, Galton, M and Robinson, S (1996) Teachers' assessments of primary children's classroom work in the creative arts. *Educational Research*, 38(2) p199-211

Hennessey, B (1994) The consensual assessment technique: An examination of the relationship between ratings of product and process creativity. *Creativity Research Journal* 7(2) p193-208

Hennessey, B and Amabile, T (1999) Consensual assessment, In M Runco (ed) *Encyclopedia of Creativity Volume 1.* San Diego: Academic Press p347-359

Hickey, M (2001) An application of Amabile's consensual assessment technique for rating the creativity of children's musical compositions. *Journal of Research in Music Education* 49(3) p234-244

Hsu, Y, Tsai, C and Chen, M (2002) A pilot study on mathematical creative analogy activities with networked peer assessment (in Chinese). *Journal of Taiwan Normal University: Mathematics and Science Education* 47(2) p1-13

Jeffrey, B and Craft, A (2004) Teaching creatively and teaching for creativity: distinctions and relationships. *Educational Studies* 30(1) p77-87

Kaufman, J, Gentile, C and Baer, J (2005) Do gifted student writers and creative writing experts rate creativity the same way? *The Gifted Child Quarterly* 49(3), p260-269

Lin, S (2005) Music arranging ability of fifth-graders: An application of Art PROPEL curriculum model (in Chinese). *Research in Arts Education* 10 p87-126

Lubart, T (1999) Creativity across cultures. In R Sternberg (ed) *Handbook of Creativity*. New York: Cambridge University Press p339-350

Niu, W and Sternberg, R (2001) Cultural influences on artistic creativity and its evaluation. *International Journal of Psychology* 36(4) p225-241

Policastro, E and Gardner, H (1995) Naive judgment and expert assessment: a critique of the attributional perspective. *Creativity Research Journal* 8(4), p391-395

Priest, T (2006) Self-evaluation, creativity, and musical achievement. *Psychology of Music* 34(1), p47-61

Qu, X and Shi, J (2005) Evaluation and reward effect on verbal creativity of field dependent-independent children. *Chinese Mental Health Journal* 19(6) p408-412

Runco, M (1996) Personal creativity: definition and developmental issues. *New Directions for Child Development* 72 p3-30

Sternberg, R J and Lubart, T I (1999) The concept of creativity: Prospects and paradigms. In Sternberg, R J (ed) *Handbook of Creativity*. Cambridge: University Press

Wolfradt, U and Pretz, J (2001) Individual differences in creativity: personality, story writing and hobbies. *European Journal of Personality* 15 p297-310

CONCLUDING REMARKS
The edges of the map?

Anna Craft, Teresa Cremin, Pamela Burnard

This volume sought to ink in and extend the edges of the map of creative learning in children aged 3-11, and how we document it. So how do the contributions in this volume extend our understanding of the what, how and why of these twin dimensions?

Our authors chose contrasting entry points to this collective and exploratory story. Each occupies a position on a spectrum, at one end of which is the theoretical account and at the other, the empirical. The theoretical perspectives offer analysis of the concept in different cultural contexts including England (Barnes *et al* and Spendlove and Wyse), the Gulf States (Al-Horr), Turkey (Oral) and the USA (Kaufman and Baer). Empirical studies spanning the spectrum of qualitative to quantitative approaches were undertaken by practitioner researchers (Churchill and Dower, Gabel-Dunk, Mardell *et al* and Smyth) and also by university-based researchers (Chappell, Craft *et al*, Cheng, Jeffrey, Sarsani, Vong and Wong) and a mixture (Burgess-Macey and Lowenthal).

Some (Chappell, Churchill and Dower, Gabel-Dunk, Smyth) are rooted in specific curriculum areas, others are more generalised (Craft *et al*, Mardell *et al*). They span a large terrain, from a focus on creative learning in and through the arts (Burgess-Macey and Loewenthal, Chappell, Gabel-Dunk, Smyth), to notions of creative learning as generalised and skill-based (Craft *et al*), and encompassed the argument that creative learning can be seen as a mixture of skill and domain based (Kaufman and Baer): a mix of perspectives and foci.

A theme running through many chapters is the nurturing environment, particularly for young children. It is highlighted in several cultures by Churchill Dower, Jeffrey and Burgess-Macey and Loewenthal, and the establishment of a respectful democratic community of learners is discussed by Mardell *et al* and by Gabel-Dunk. A further theme is the significance of the aesthetic dimension in children's learning and in pedagogy.

In terms of expanding the map, the most striking aspect of this collection is the sheer breadth of approaches to understanding creative learning. It goes far beyond the partnership-based approach encouraged by the English project Creative Partnerships, discussed in the Introduction, which framed the term 'creative learning' in a way that took hold in and beyond Britain.

Creativity is also related to culture in the sense of heritage and tradition in a much broader sense, by several authors such as Oral, who discusses the evolution of creativity through culture, policies and the evolution of teacher characteristics; a case of meme complex (Dawkins, 2000). Vong, too, discusses creative learning in relation to much wider cultural values in China, highlighting distinct differences between government-based policy statements and an eastern tradition which values conformity, hierarchy and didactic approaches to teaching and learning. This theme is echoed in Sarsani's discussion of teachers' views of creativity in India, and in Cheng's discussion on creative learning in Hong Kong. Wong's study highlights the cultural tensions encountered by Hong Kong teachers who seek to foster creative engagement, and the difficulties faced by early childhood education leaders. Arguing that creative learning has an important place in education, Al-Horr explores the tensions within the GCC states between this ideal and pervading religion-based traditions and beliefs.

Jeffrey draws on the creative learning criteria of ownership, control, innovation and relevance from a comparative perspective. He draws on his work with Woods to highlight differences in the ways in which various European cultures foster creative learning (Jeffrey and Woods, 2003). He argues that the focus in England, Scotland and Ireland on explicit policy making, which seeks explicitly to foster creativity in education, contrasts with Spain and Austria where the culture of performative values is emphasised. And yet he notes with some irony that teacher artistry or creativity is much more prevalent in Spain and Austria, with roots far back into educational philosophy. This is another example of how deeply the cultural values which influence the theory and practice of creative learning are rooted. Given the cultural embeddedness of creative learning, Cheng highlights the issues involved in evaluating the extent to which the outcomes of creative learning may be creative, the act of assessment or evaluation itself being a cultural product.

Within this rather broader notion of culture than the one which spawned the term 'creative learning', our authors describe creative learning as requiring high pupil engagement and low teacher imposition, as illustrated by a variety of situations. These range from the close-up focus of children's questioning within 'possibility thinking' at the heart of creativity (Craft *et al*) and the equally close-up AKTEV model of creative learning involving auditory, kinaesthetic, tactile, emotional and visual elements (Smyth), to the proposal of a more encompassing and holistic understanding of teacher and pupil activity in creative learning (Barnes *et al*).

Even so, the term creative learning remains problematic, because there is no consensus about its meaning. Although widespread in England, it is not so pervasively used elsewhere. This point is made by Sarsani, in relation to Indian teachers' perspectives, and by Al-Horr from the stance of the GGC.

There is similar difficulty over the term 'documenting' creative learning, which has crept into international discourse from the Reggio Emilia pre-schools of Northern Italy, where careful written, pictorial and audio documentation is seen almost as an act of love (*Harvard University Gazette*, 2001, Rinaldi, 2006).

The process of documenting is now used in England and beyond, particularly in the early years of learning. Government policy in England emphasises the significance of documenting individual and group learning for early years practitioners in particular: this is in order to observe, assess and plan appropriately, using cameras, post-its, children's own notes and drawings, and also sound recording (DfES, 2007).

The authors in this book draw on a wide range of documentation, ranging from the need to support children's next steps in learning, to documentation which allows one or more people to reflect on learning together, to documentation which is effectively research data. In his chapter on research methods, Martin recognises the potential of the varied approaches which are brought to enquiry into creative learning. There is still much potential for development. Documenting creative learning might involve studies which involve more creative methodologies in participatory research *with* children.

Some of the definitions are about who is involved in the documentation as well as what is documented and how; images on the jacket of this book include work being developed with primary school children in the South West of England, to develop their skills as documentors (Walton and Barefoot, 2007). To what extent might the process of documentation be extended further, with children taking on key roles in not only collecting but also reflecting on, evidence of learning? Some of the authors demonstrate that this can be done. Through closely engaging with children in the reflective process, others reach towards some of the metacognitive benefits which come from doing so (Gabel-Dunk, Mardell *et al*).

Considering the age of the children with whom adults tend to approach documenting creative learning, seems long overdue. For whilst early years practitioners are perhaps familiar with the notion of documenting learning in order to appropriately stimulate the next creative or generative learning engagement, this aspect of pedagogy may be less familiar to teachers of older children. Does the education system itself compel children to suppress their creativity in the later primary years? Recent research work undertaken to explore progression in creative learning (Craft *et al*, 2006) suggests this may be the case. If so, how can the ways in which practitioners frame creative learning and its documentation alter this situation?

As Feldman predicts in his Foreword, in mapping creative learning and how we foster it, there remains a great deal to do. We continue to design and build not just one aeroplane but several, as we test fly them across an expanding territory. And this invites more work in each of the three areas we set out to explore in this book, as follows.

Considering the 'what'

This collection offers a range of perspectives on creative learning which slip between and perhaps at times conflate 'creative teaching' and some notion of child-initiated and 'owned' learning. Offering international evidence of what creative learning might be, each contributor relates to different assumptions about the nature of creativity and the nature of learning within different domains. Comparative research is needed to explore what can be learned from closer articulation between studies in developmental psychology, neuroscience, and specific disciplines and inter-disciplinary contexts, in order to afford the 'learning' in creative learning deeper and broader purchase. There is also a need to consider broader goals for creative learning, connecting these to learning futures in and beyond schools, in an age of innovation.

Extending further what documenting creative learning could involve in terms of how it is integral to teaching and learning, and what means are used not only to record but also to interpret documentation, is also vital. This development work would expand the spectrum of documentation which spans 'noting' at one end to analysis and research at the other.

174

Extending how we foster and document creative learning

There seems, then, a clear need to extend the 'how' in both creative learning and its documentation so as to address the tensions between ideal and actual. Systemic changes in learning systems in an age of innovation where flexibility, imagination, capacity to recognise possibilities and transform what is to what might be, are increasingly vital for survival. Such qualities are increasingly what schools and early years settings have to foster effectively.

There is also a clear need to extend our methodology in documentation, adopting more innovative approaches to researching children's ideas, experiences and their engagement in and measurement of creative learning. The scope is enormous for practitioner research in tracking how creative learning can evolve, its progression across and between the years of schooling, its effectiveness and its outcomes. We need to expand the analysis of what we collect, paying attention to how teachers and children could be involved in this research, together with others from beyond the classroom. Innovative attempts to explore new models are under way through the Creative Partnerships programme in England (eg Craft and Chappell, 2007; Craft *et al*, 2007a), and through the Creative Action Research Awards (CARA) programme, engaging cultural partners and children as researchers alongside teachers and university based research staff (Craft *et al*, 2007b). More is needed.

Extending the 'why'

We have important questions to pose around the values base of creativity in education, which we tend to assume is 'a good thing'. Whilst undoubtedly a case can be made for creative learning in offering readiness for a global market economy, we can also ask, like Craft *et al* (in press), how we can foster creativity wisely, in paying attention to the ends and not only the means. Thus we might scrutinise the purposes to which creative learning is put more closely, which in turn may influence how we document it.

We argued in the Introduction that the discourse of creative learning was opened by the Creative Partnerships initiative in England. Throughout the book the authors have shown how the notion of creative learning opens up ways of exploring the boundaries of creativity in education, how it is defined, where and why it is seen as relevant, how it is fostered, why it is documented in specific ways in different contexts. Whilst partnership with the cultural and creative sector may form a partial context for these boundary explorations, this is only one of many dimensions waiting to be explored further.

References

Craft, A, Gardner, H and Claxton, G (eds) (in press) *Creativity, Wisdom and Trusteeship: exploring the role of education.* Thousand Oaks: Corwin Press

Craft, A, Grainger, T, Burnard, P and Chappell, K (2006) *Progression in Creative Learning (PICL Pilot): A study funded by Creative Partnerships* http://www.creative-partnerships.com/researchand evaluation/researchAndEvaluationProjects (May 2007)

Craft, A. and Chappell, K. (2007) Fostering possibility through co-researching creative movement with 7-11 year-olds. Paper presented at *Imaginative Education Research Group Symposium*, Simon Fraser University, Vancouver, Canada, July 2007

Craft, A., Best, P. and Dillon, P. (2007a) Creativity and the Outdoors: perspectives of pupils and teachers in a North of England primary school. Paper presented at *17th European Conference of European Early Childhood Research Association* (EECERA), Prague, August 2007

Craft, A, Chappell, K and Best, P (2007) *Analysis of the Creativity Action Research Awards Two (CARA 2) Programme: Final Report.* October 2007

Dawkins, R (2000) Selfish Genes and Selfish Memes. In D R Hofstadter and D C Dennett (eds) *Mind's Eye.* New York: Basic Books

Department for Education and Skills (2007) Observation, Assessment and Learning. http://www.standards.dfes.gov.uk/ePDs/eyfs/eyfs_website/resources/transcripts/documenting-learning.htm

Harvard University Gazette, December 13th (2001) http://www.hno.harvard.edu/gazette/2001/12.13/10-projectzero.html

Jeffrey, B and Woods, P (2003), *The Creative School: A framework for success, quality and effectiveness.* London: Routledge/Falmer

Rinaldi, C (2006) *In dialogue with Reggio Emilia: Listening, researching and learning.* London: Routledge

Walton, K and Barefoot, S (2007) New Generation Documentors http://kaminawalton.co.uk/action.html (May 2007)

Glossary of abbreviated terms

AKTEV Imagination Repertoire: auditory, kinaesthetic, tactile, emotional and visual elements of creative learning (see chapter by Smyth)

APT – Amusement Park Theory (See chapter by Kaufman and Baer)

Atlas-ti – commercial data analysis package for qualitative analysis of large amounts of data including graphical, audio, video and textual

BCRAC – Bradford County Regional Arts Council based in Pennsylvania, USA, working works in partnership with families to tackle issues through creative learning programmes in order to break cycles of deprivation

CARA – Creative Action Research Awards run by CapeUK for Creative Partnerships in England

CapeUK – an independent research and development agency based in England focusing on creativity and learning, especially creative partnership

CAT – Consensual Assessment Technique, devised by Amabile (See chapter by Cheng)

CLASS – Specialist Schools and Academies Trust Creative Learning and Specialist Subjects project

CLASP – Creative Learning and Student Perspectives research project, 2002-2004, funded by European Commission and ESRC (see Jeffrey and Craft *et al* chapters)

DCSF – Department for Children, Schools and Families (England)

DCMS – Department for Culture, Media and Sport (England)

DfEE – Department for Education and Employment (England)

DfES – Department for Education and Skills (England)

D/T – Design and technology

EPCS – Eliot Pearson Children's School

ESRC – Economic and Social Research Council (United Kingdom)

GCC – Gulf Corporation Council

MAGIC – a process that motivates children to associate, generate, innovate and communicate ideas (see chapter by Smyth)

NACCCE – National Advisory Committee on Creative and Cultural Education, 1999 (England)

NCSL – National College for School Leadership (England)

NVivo – commercial computer-based package for analysis of qualitative text-based data

Ofsted – Office for Standards in Education (England)

PICL – Progression in Creative Learning research project (see chapters by Chappell, also Spendlove and Wyse)

PNS – Primary National Strategy

PRAXIS III – a systematic system for observation of a teacher's instruction through analysis of video-based classroom interaction, using 19 specific criteria in four behavioural domains, each based on research about teacher behaviours as they relate to effective classrooms. Developed by Educational Testing Service in New Jersey (1994) (see chapter by David Martin)

QCA – Qualifications and Curriculum Authority (England)

UNICEF – The United Nations International Children's Emergency Fund

Author Index

179

Subject Index